2.99

THE GIFT OF GIVING

R. T. Kendall

Hodder & Stoughton
LONDON SYDNEY AUCKLAND

To every Church leader

Copyright © 1982 by R. T. Kendall

First published in Great Britain 1982. This edition 1998

This right of R. T. Kendall to be identified as the Author of the Work has been asserted by him in accordance with the Copyright, Designs and Patents Act 1988.

10 9 8 7 6 5 4

British Library Cataloguing in Publication Data
A record for this book is available from the British Library

ISBN 0 340 72156 1

Printed and bound in Great Britain by
Clays Ltd, St Ives plc

Hodder and Stoughton
A division of Hodder Headline Ltd
338 Euston Road
London NW1 3BH

A Word from Philip Hacking

This new edition of R. T. Kendall's book was never more needed than in the church of today. In part that is because of the crying need for more systematic and biblical giving in the local church and spilling out to the missionary work of the church. Every sensitive pastor is aware of desperate needs in the world and the inability to meet them.

But this book is even more relevant because it is not just a challenge to giving, it is an example of how to base your teaching on giving from biblical exposition. I want to applaud the major thesis of the book, which is that tithing is basically for the local church. If every church member heeded this, there would be no financial worries in any missionary society around the globe. R.T. manages skilfully to avoid falling into the prosperity gospel net. The promises of Scripture are wonderful and not to be despised, but there is always a danger of encouraging giving for selfish ends.

This book is vital for young Christians looking at the reality of their commitment. It is also a very helpful exercise for mature Christians. It may not make pleasant reading but it certainly could open a new vista at a time when there are so many possibilities if only Christians take their consecration practically and seriously. Not least, the book is down-to-earth and faces some of the practical questions that a reader wants to address to the author and so rarely can.

I like the new title because it reminds us that tithing is a privilege and not just an obligation.

Contents

Foreword

I believe in giving. I believe in giving tithes to the local church, alms to the poor and offerings for God's work around the world.

Though I have been a missionary for over twenty-four years, I have enjoyed giving as a way of life. I was taught to give by those who discipled me as a young Christian. They reminded me that God himself is generous – He gives mercy, grace and forgiveness. He gave His own son. 'Will He not give us all things with Him?' (Romans 8:32)

As a growing Christian it was explained to me that Christ-like generosity was a character trait that was to affect all areas of my relationships with other people. So it was a very natural thing for my wife and I, as a newly married couple, to share the resources that God entrusted to us. Though we only averaged $5,500 annual income for the first four years we were married, we gave over a third of that away each year!

The amazing thing is, all of our needs were met. We never lacked food, clothes or transportation. That is not to say that there were not times that we did not wonder where the next meal was coming from!

I looked a long time for this book. When I arrived in Holland in 1973 my commitment to generosity and giving was tested deeply. Some Dutch friends informed me that, since I was an American, I should not discuss money, nor ask people to give to our work. The first few times this happened I did not take it too seriously. But when people said this at almost every Christian meeting I attended, I began to become concerned.

As I prayed about this I began to sense that this was not a

cultural issue, but a biblical one. I also sensed that there was idolatry in the hearts of many believers concerning money. I know this sounds a bit rash, but I had a deep concern for the Church of Jesus Christ. I sensed many were not free to give of their resources in a joyful manner.

I decided to use every opportunity I had to teach on finances. When I was given the opportunity I would take an offering, not for my own organisation, but for other ministries, local churches, Christian ministers, missionaries and evangelists.

I looked for opportunities to teach people to give. Nobody could accuse me of doing that for myself. I was doing it for others. I was trying to set an example of how God wanted the Body of Christ to enjoy the blessing, worship and joy of following the example of our Lord in cultivating the gift of giving.

Dutch Christians responded wonderfully. I know of no more generous nation on the face of the earth. I learned through the experience that God wants Christian leaders to tackle this sensitive area of stewardship and so glorify Christ. We are not to hold back out of fear of what the people we lead will say about our motives. We have a responsibility to teach what God's word says about all of our pockets.

I commend this book to you. It is simple, short and profound. It touches on an area that will affect every person's life, and it does so in a forthright, biblical and Christ-like manner. I believe it will be an aid to many leaders in teaching their people, and will help many Christians understand the freedom and joy that there is in obeying God's word on the subject of Christian stewardship and tithing.

Floyd McClung

Preface

A few years ago my wife and I found ourselves at one of Gerald Coates' Christmas parties. I spotted Gerald Williams, the TV tennis commentator. Waiting for someone to introduce me (trying to be British) I discerned few there who knew me, so I got the courage to approach him and I introduced myself. He looked at me and said, 'I owe you an apology'. 'Do you know me?' He replied, 'You taught me to tithe. I should have written you by now.' He said he bought my book *Tithing* in a Brighton bookstore. 'After reading two chapters I wrote out my first cheque and I've been tithing ever since.'

I asked to write this book. I felt there was a need for it. I knew of no book on this subject. But I said to Hodders, 'I will only write it if you keep the price under £1.00'. They eventually agreed but they, too, attached a condition: that Westminster Chapel would purchase 1,000 copies in advance! They feared that there would not be much demand for this book. But we agreed. That was nearly ten years ago.

After I finished writing I let some of my friends read the manuscript and they graciously gave commendations, some of which appear on the back cover. The result was that I had my first (and only) best-seller! *Tithing* went into a half dozen or more reprints but it went out of print two or three years ago.

My publisher decided to re-issue the same book under a new title and cover. Sorry about the price! Floyd McClung and Philip Hacking have kindly provided commendations. I hope this venture will not merely give the book new life but will engender fresh life in many churches and believers. For tithing will do something quite wonderful for the person who begins and continues to give God what is His.

I have heard many stories that have resulted from this book. Perhaps the most striking was that of an Anglican layman who used his tithe to purchase copies of *Tithing* for every member of his parish! The consequence was that the giving doubled in that church the first month!

I have felt no need to change a single word. If you bought this under the new title, having already purchased the old one, and discover too late there is no difference, I hope you will forgive us! Just read it again – or give it away!

London   R. T. Kendall
September 1991

Introduction

I doubt that there is a more threatening subject than that of tithing. That which touches our wallets and purses taps a very sensitive nerve. Frank M. Hubbard sums it up rather bluntly: 'When a fellow says, "It ain't the money but the principle of the thing," it's the money.' Voltaire went so far as to say, 'When it is a question of money, everybody is of the same religion.'

Was Voltaire right? I hope not. And yet it is strange how uneasy we feel when the matter of *giving* emerges. Many of us, however, would prefer to speak of giving than of *tithing*. Talk of giving makes us nervous but the idea of tithing arouses feelings of hostility in us. Our immediate reaction is often to dismiss it as either 'bringing in the Law' or, at least, the classic example of a minister who has 'quit preaching and gone to meddling'.

The purpose of this book is to make what is threatening thrilling. It may well be a book that will change your life. If you are a tither already you will warm to this theme. If you are not a tither, this book is for you. My hope of convincing you is that 1. you are a Christian; 2. you really want to please the Lord; and 3. you want to be governed by the Bible.

A Solution Nobody Talks About

Tithing is a solution nobody talks about. Solution to what? Answer: many more problems indeed than many have thought. If every professing Christian would tithe, every congregation would be free of financial worries and could begin truly to be 'the salt of the earth' (Matt. 5:13). If every Christian would tithe the Church would begin to make an impact on the world that could change it. The Church instead is paralysed. Tithing Christians could make a big difference.

But because most Christians do not tithe, the Church remains in a generally discouraged state. It struggles to pay its own bills: electricity, water, heat, pastor's salary. Perhaps the Church will do something about redecorating its premises or improving the manse if there is any extra. In the meantime money that might go to missions has to be kept at home: a handful of the faithful carry on most Christian work with precious little money.

The world is unimpressed with the Church because the Church has not commanded the world's attention and respect. When we do not support the work of God according to the pattern that is set down in the Bible it should not surprise us that the world does not respect us. Why should they, when we don't respect God—or His way? We show how much we care by how much we give. If religion has not touched our cheque books, then Voltaire got it right. I fear that many, many Christians have vindicated Voltaire's statement.

It need not be that way. It must not. For a good number of Christians it is not. There are many Christians who *do* tithe. They do not need this book but perhaps will enjoy it most. Many of you who read this may well wish I had interviewed you that you might have given your own testimony.

Apart from solving the Church's financial problems that it might be released to change the world, tithing is a solution to one's own spiritual problem. Question: have you wished that you might truly grow in grace? Are you struggling with the same old trials and temptations? Are you still suffering from a feeling of barrenness? Have you wondered why there has been minimal development in your own understanding over the years?

Why do I raise questions like this? Because it is very likely that a big hitch in your Christian growth has to do with fidelity in stewardship of money. Sooner or later every Christian comes face to face with the use of his money. And what happens then? Either he will squarely and honestly face his Christian responsibility or he will draw back. If he draws back from this responsibility it is not likely that anything he does will work or compensate for this refusal to come to grips with the stewardship of money.

Jesus said: 'He that is faithful in that which is least is faithful also in much' (Luke 16:10). In other words, trying to by-pass (or move beyond) 'the least' is sheer folly. It is playing games with ourselves. It is trying to go from A to Z by passing over the other letters of the alphabet. We cannot get to Z until we have moved from A to B, etc. The matter of stewardship of money is fundamental to Christian growth. If we come face to face with the 'light' God gives us with respect to our use of money, we must walk in that light (1 John 1:7); to refuse to do so has awesome consequences. 'If therefore the light that is in thee be darkness, how great is that darkness!' (Matt. 5:23). Not to walk in the light results in an arrested development at the spiritual level. (Sometimes this arrested development may be experienced at other levels—psychological, physical, even financial.) This arrested development is like a blind spot. Like Balaam's ass, you cannot move beyond no matter how hard you try (see Numbers 22:22ff).

To put it another way: who among us at one time or another has not sought to use one form of obedience (or righteous deed) to offset a deficiency in another area? 'I don't tithe but I go to church three times a week.' 'I don't tithe but I bring people to church.' 'I don't tithe but I read my Bible and pray more than most people do.' Etc., etc.

Does it work? No, it does not. We who do 'more' when we are aware of some form of disobedience in our Christian lives are not talking to God but ourselves. We really project upon God what we hope He is thinking. It is nothing but playing games with God—and ourselves.

We are all guilty of this, however. We compare ourselves to others—that is, to those who make us look slightly better. A friend of mine, a minister in Britain, told me of a trip he made to America. The first week he was there he stayed with some Christian friends who seemed to want to talk a lot about Christians who smoke or drink. 'Isn't it awful,' so they would

go on, 'that some people call themselves Christians who use
tobacco or take an alcoholic beverage?' My friend would
patiently and politely let them go on and on. He admitted
that he was rather glad to go to another place to have a
different host. My friend and his wife then flew to Grand
Rapids where they were met by a Dutch Calvinist who
smoked a cigar on the way from the airport and offered them
an alcoholic beverage as soon as they got home. They could
not help but notice the contrast between the two Christian
atmospheres.

But that is not the end of the story. The following Sunday
night after the church service they were driving down a main
street in Grand Rapids in which there was a famous restaurant. My friend spoke up, 'Look! There's a Howard
Johnson's Restaurant. Do you suppose we could stop and get
some of their ice cream?' Silence. Reluctantly the driver of
the car pulled into the parking lot of this restaurant. They
went inside but there was silence between them.

'Is everything all right?' my friend asked.

'Yes,' replied the subdued Dutchman.

'No, it isn't,' insisted my friend. 'Something is bothering
you.'

'Well,' this man finally responded, 'this is Sunday—the
Sabbath, and we do not buy on the Sabbath.'

When my minister friend and his wife were alone in their
room he said to her, 'It seems that everybody has got to have
something they are against. I wonder what it is with us?'

So with all of us. We try to secure a righteous feeling about
one area in which we are at home in order to relieve ourselves
of any guilt that might emerge in another. 'I might smoke a
cigar now and then, but I don't eat in a restaurant on
Sunday.' 'I might eat in a restaurant on Sunday, but I don't
smoke or drink.' 'I might watch a movie on television, but I
wouldn't go into a public cinema.' 'I might not be a tither,
but I neither smoke, drink, go to cinemas, watch a movie on
television, or buy a Sunday newspaper!' Is such a person
better off? Not really. In some ways he is worse off, because
his 'righteousnesses' blind him to any further need.

Let not the reader surmise that I am saying that tithing is the final solution. For it is equally possible to say, 'I may not attend church on Sunday nights or witness very much—but I do tithe.' This person would let tithing blind him as much as anything else could. It seems that all of us seek for that which gives us a quasi-righteous feeling. The tither is vulnerable too. Let nobody think that by solution I am suggesting that being a tither means 'you're there'. Not at all.

But I am saying this. Sooner or later everyone must face up to his responsibility as a Christian steward of money. Stewardship of money pertains to areas other than tithing of course, but tithing has got to be faced in this connection. We cannot avoid the problem. How we respond to the light that God throws on our paths when it comes may well determine then and there whether or not we are given more light in which to walk. For if we do not walk in the light that God kindly sheds on our paths and on our minds and in our hearts it is not likely we will get further light for other matters. 'But if we walk in the light, as he is in the light, we have fellowship one with another, and the blood of Jesus Christ his Son cleanseth us from all sin' (1 John 1:7). This is another way of saying he that is faithful in that which is least will be faithful also in much. What is more presumptuous than praying for more light from God when we are not walking in the light we already have?

By *solution*, then, I mean this. Apart from the fact that were all Christians to tithe it would solve the Church's financial problems, I am sure that becoming a tither provides a definite breakthrough for every Christian. It unlocks the door of his mind, heart and will. It releases. It emancipates. It frees. Becoming a tither is a milestone in a Christian's life.

In some cases a person begins tithing as soon as he becomes a Christian. I watched Dr D. James Kennedy lead a man to Christ in the man's home in Fort Lauderdale. This man had been a church member in Ohio for years but had never been truly converted. That evening the man was wonderfully saved. As we walked toward the door at the close of that memorable evening, the man said, 'Oh, by the way, I

want to start tithing. Should I tithe the gross or the net?'
Conversion did it in this case. But with some Christians
tithing is a post-conversion commitment. When this happens
it can be like a second conversion. There is a release from
within that is very liberating and pleasant indeed. One
would no more think of not tithing from then on than he
would think of doing anything else that would displease the
Lord. This release is not only a feeling of peace and rest but a
grace to do things with more vigour than ever before—
whether it be effectiveness on the job or understanding the
Bible.

In other words, tithing does something for you *spiritually*.
You will only ask, 'Why did I not start tithing sooner?' It
does something for you that cannot be explained in terms of
material return. It sets you on a course to become more than
you have been—more what God wants you to be, more of
what you are naturally capable of being. Tithing is so
essential to your development as a Christian that nothing
will be its adequate substitute.

Why is this? Because tithing is as much a part of Christian
gratitude and obedience as any commandment God ever
gave. We are so made that until God has all of us we are
unhappy with ourselves. Augustine put it like this: 'Thou
hast made us for Thyself; our hearts are restless until they
find their rest in Thee.' So it is with tithing—sooner or later.
We are made to respond graciously to God. This response, if
it does not affect our cheque books, is very minute indeed.
Tithing is God's way. Until we are consistently, regularly
and faithfully tithing there is something defective about our
Christian life that will not be remedied by any other form of
Christian obedience. But when that area of obedience *is* dealt
with, the reward is wonderful indeed.

Reward is possibly not the right word. It seems at first that
the blessing should be called reward. But the time is likely to
come that one sees the reward as tithing itself—not the
blessing that emerges from doing it but merely doing it!
It works like this. At first we are like babies, or children,
who need reinforcement and encouragement. But there is a

stage in which a Christian doesn't even look at it that way; he thanks God for the privilege of tithing. Tithing, then, becomes its own reward. In fact it becomes hard to tell the difference between giving cheerfully and giving selfishly.

Someone may say: 'Surely one would be tithing with a wrong motive if he does it for reward.' I answer: who among us is so godly and spiritual that he is impervious to any kind of promise of blessing? Who among us can do *anything* indefinitely without some kind of encouragement from God? Who can pray daily and faithfully for many days without there being *some* token of God's smile? All of us need encouragement. God knows this. 'O taste and see that the Lord is good' (Ps. 34:8). 'I will sing unto the Lord, because he hath dealt bountifully with me' (Ps. 13:6). 'Bless the Lord, O my soul, and forget not all his benefits' (Ps. 103:2).

God preserves us from being demoralised by stepping in—sometimes only in the nick of time. God is never too late, never too early, but He is always just on time. Even though God would not have to promise a blessing if we obey, He always does. He deserves our obedience with or without any blessing. But the truth is, God *never* demands obedience without a promise of blessing. 'For he knoweth our frame; he remembereth that we are dust' (Ps. 103:14).

Obey Him. He will bless you. He loves to bless you. This is the way He is with His own. Our obedience moves His heart. He is touched by our gratitude. He cannot hide how He feels. He lets us know it. Here is the principle: you cannot *out-do* the Lord.

So with tithing. You cannot out-give the Lord. He loves to bless those who honour Him in this way. Dr James H. Milby, now living in Tennessee, has recently retired from being chairman of the board of one of the largest life insurance companies in America. My parents and other relatives have known him for years and can recall the poverty-like conditions in which he was brought up in Springfield, Illinois. Not long ago I spent a day with him bonefishing in the Florida Keys.

I asked him: 'What is the key to your success as a businessman?'

He said, 'The answer to that is very simple. Many years ago I made a contract with the Lord, claiming the promise: "Them that honour me I will honour" (1 Sam. 2:30). I began tithing.' He went on to say he began tithing when he had almost no income, even when he could not 'afford' to tithe. But he kept his 'contract' with the Lord. God began blessing him as he went from one level of business to another. Those who know him best are aware not only of his business acumen but his bold witness for the Lord Jesus Christ. Dr and Mrs Milby supported us with their prayers and financial support when we moved from America to study at Oxford. They paid every penny of my tuition at Oxford University. When Dr Milby made his 'contract' with the Lord over fifty years ago he did not envisage the kind of prosperity that came. He took 1 Samuel 2:30 seriously, however. I am only one of many who have been blessed by the Milbys like this.

For tithing is not only a solution for the *Church* at a financial level; there is no reason to question that it applies also to the *individual* this way. Perhaps not everyone will go to the top of management or of industry or of anything else that suggests a greater prosperity. But we do have a number of rather plain statements that suggest you cannot out-give God—even with reference to material return. 'He which soweth sparingly shall reap also sparingly; and he which soweth bountifully shall reap also bountifully' (2 Corinthians 9:6). 'Bring ye all the tithes into the storehouse, that there may be meat in mine house, and prove me now herewith, saith the Lord of hosts, if I will not open you the windows of heaven, and pour you out a blessing that there shall not be room enough to receive it. And I will rebuke the devourer for your sakes, and he shall not destroy the fruits of your ground; neither shall your vine cast her fruit before the time in the field, saith the Lord of hosts' (Malachi 3:10–11).

These promises clearly point to a *material* return as one kind of blessing from the Lord. Obviously some will prosper more than others, owing to gifts, place of responsibility, or opportunity. But *at bottom* is a promise for *all* believers that they will be honoured even at a material level in such a way that, whether it be more or less than others, it is more than it would have been had they not been faithful in Christian stewardship. There are countless testimonies which could be brought forward that tell of financial hardships, debt and distress, until tithing was begun. Not that such people became millionaires or drove Rolls-Royces, but they lived without the terror of constant financial adversity.

Why some Christians don't tithe

There are various reasons that Christians don't tithe. Perhaps we could ask ten different people why they do not tithe and get ten different answers. But here are three basic reasons.

1. *Some Christians do not tithe because they simply have not been taught to tithe.* In this case their not being tithers is largely owing to the failure of the ministry they have been sitting under. As with the hearing of the Gospel so with the teaching of tithing; we must hear in order to believe, and we must be taught in order to know the way. 'How then shall they call on him in whom they have not believed? and how shall they believe in him of whom they have not heard? and how shall they hear without a preacher?' (Rom. 10:14). As we cannot become Christians unless we have heard the Gospel so we are not going to tithe unless we are taught first.

To put it slightly differently: tithing is not something which comes 'naturally' to any of us. Perhaps I should share with the reader how I became a tither. I feel most fortunate indeed that I was given a head start on this matter. I was taught it at home. My father was a convinced tither. (Whether my father learned it at home or from his minister I do not know, but whoever taught him taught him well!) I would say that the best place to learn tithing is at home. I am thankful that I not only was born into a Christian home but also a tithing home. I would urge the reader to teach your son or daughter to tithe. You do them a great favour to lay before them this wonderful Biblical teaching. You certainly do them no favour to let them grow up and begin making money without knowing that the tithe is the Lord's. They may not like it, mind you, when you urge them to begin tithing when they are still under your roof. I certainly didn't.

My first paying job (at age ten) was selling an American newspaper door-to-door. It was a weekly newspaper called *Grit*. My father said that he sold *Grit* when he was a boy, and what was good enough for him was good enough for me! This paper sold then for ten cents a copy and I made three cents every time I persuaded any neighbour within three blocks of our house to buy one. The first week I actually made fifty cents. I was so happy with myself! How thrilling it was to earn money on my own and not merely to have an 'allowance' from my parents.

My father however had to get into the act and when I was counting my money on the dining-room table he had the impertinence to put his finger on a nickel—and slid it to one side. 'That, my son, is the Lord's.'

I reached for that nickel faster than you can bat an eyelash and brought it back to the forty-five cents. 'That is mine,' I replied. 'I earned it. I worked hard for it.'

'No, son,' my father retorted sticking to his guns, 'that is the Lord's.' 'But Dad . . .'

That was my introduction to tithing. But I've never been sorry. My father is not a minister but a faithful layman—a preacher's dream if there ever was one. He would not dream of giving to God one cent (the equivalent to a ½p in Britain) less than the full 10% of his income—no matter the source of that income. My parents were never wealthy—far from it. But my father had this strange idea that God has a way of making the 90% that we keep to ourselves up to or even above the 100%—and withholding 10% of that would be stealing God's money.

It is a very great deprivation indeed not to be told about tithing. Your own minister does you a great favour in putting this teaching before you—regularly, firmly and clearly. The problem in many churches is that a minister is afraid that his people will be suspicious of his motives. I understand and sympathise with this. When a minister is already underpaid (and most of them are) and then begins to preach on tithing one can well understand why such a minister would feel uneasy.

I would say that the answer to this dilemma is that if such a minister really does believe in tithing God will not only honour such preaching and teaching but will remove people's suspicions. The people we regularly preach to can see pretty well right through us anyway and can tell what our real motives are. When we preach with conviction they have little difficulty seeing this.

2. *Some Christians do not tithe because of a misunderstanding of the place of God's Law in the Bible.* The moment one raises verses such as 'the tithe is the Lord's' (Lev. 27:30), or 'Will a man rob God?' (Mal. 3:8) someone else is usually around who says, 'But that's the Old Testament. We are not under the Law but under grace.'

A special section of this book is devoted to this matter. I suspect however that those whose rationale for not tithing is on theological grounds are not all that anxious to tithe anyway. I don't want to be unkind, but do these people really believe they are glorifying God by not tithing? Is it not rather a way of escape for them? Are they not hoping in any case that tithing is an antiquated enterprise so that they need not face the matter?

There are sincere Christians who have been influenced at this point but who can be guided safely into a lucid Biblical understanding of the Law. I make this promise: a clear understanding of the Law is not only a deterrent to legalism but is positively emancipating from legalism. Those who truly want to be guided by the New Testament (our starting point) will find great joy and warmth by what the Apostle Paul has to say about this. Not only will this encourage the believer to tithe but, even more importantly, will lead that Christian into a deeper sense of freedom and assurance.

But is not the very word 'tithe' an Old Testament term? Yes. Nearly everything we as Christians believe originated in the Old Testament. Words like 'faith', 'atonement', 'redemption', 'righteousness', 'sin', etc., have their origin in the Old Testament. *But not in the Law.* The big mistake we so often make is that we say—if it is in the Old Testament it must be under the Law. This is wrong. 'The law is not of faith,' said Paul (Gal. 3:12). Men like Abel, Noah, Abraham, Isaac, Jacob and Joseph did what they did by *faith* (Heb. 11:4–22) and this took place *before* the Law came! Not only that; men like Moses, Joshua, Gideon, Samuel and David did what they did by *faith* (Heb. 11:23–32) and this took place *after* the Law came! The writer of the Epistle to the Hebrews would have us follow *all* these men.

Nothing is more gratifying than to see how the Old Testament and the New Testament relate to each other. And yet our starting point is the New Testament because 'the righteousness (justice) of God is revealed from faith to faith: as it is written, The just shall live by faith' (Rom. 1:17). We begin with the revelation of God's righteousness—indeed the final and full revelation of it. If we begin with the Law it is not likely we will ever get away from it, but if we begin with the Gospel we can see the Law is something which was 'added' (Gal. 3:19; Rom. 5:20—'came along side'—in the Greek).

3. *Some Christians do not tithe because they refuse to do so.* Some are convinced, others don't *want* to be convinced; but at bottom is a refusal to part with what we regard as 'ours'.

What hope is there that a book like this would help a person like that? Answer: there is a lot of hope. I speak from personal experience. I know what it is to be in a temporary state of indifference to the matter of tithing. I know what it is to be a non-tithing Christian. I know what it is to be so deep in debt that tithing seemed an utter impossibility. Shortly after my wife and I married we found ourselves plunged deep into debt. The reader would find it hard to believe how much money we owed during the first year of our marriage. I blush when I think about it. Some of the bills could not be helped, others were the consequence of imprudence on my part. At any rate, tithing was not on the agenda. I was engaged in secular work, for I was in no financial position to allow a Church to call me as minister.

I came in one day from work very, very discouraged. I fell to my knees in a sense of desperation, hoping that God would give me a ray of light that He would help me through. I walked into our dining room and there lay on the table a large white Bible my grandmother had given me. I picked it up and opened it. I didn't like what I found. Not a bit. 'Will a man rob God?' (Mal. 3:8). I just closed the Bible and sat down to watch the TV (which I still owed for).

But I was perfectly miserable. I knew that eventually I would have to go back to tithing. But I postponed this for a while longer. In the meantime things went from bad to worse. Although my wife and I were both working it seemed that paying our bills was like dipping a cup into the ocean of debt. One day I made the turn. I started tithing—despite my debts. Here is how we did it. We took 10% of our gross income right off the top—making tithing the Number One Priority. (If you don't pay your tithes that way, you will never do it!) I paid the bills with the remaining 90%. We were not out of debt in weeks but we were completely out of debt in less than two years, and those days became among the happiest we have known.

I had not been tithing because I did not want to do so. One of my deacons in a former church used to say, 'If you don't tithe, God will get it anyway.' Not that God will get it for His work but He most certainly has a way of keeping us from enjoying the entire 100%.

I fear that many do not want to be convinced. They haven't really thought it through, nor do they want to think it through. They retreat into blissful ignorance. But they are not enriched. They are impoverished.

O. S. Hawkins put it like this. 'The principal hindrance to the advancement of the Kingdom of God is greed. It is the chief obstacle to heaven-sent revival. It seems that when the back of greed is broken, the human spirit soars into regions of unselfishness. I believe it is safe to say there can be no continuous revival without "hilarious" giving. And I fear no contradiction: wherever there is "hilarious" giving there will soon be revival!'

1

WHY EVERY CHRISTIAN
SHOULD TITHE

There is ultimately only one reason why every Christian should be a tither: because it is Biblical. All other reasons, whatever their advantages may be, would not have any weight behind them at all if what we are talking about was not utterly Biblical. To put it another way: tithing is not *adiaphoron*—a 'thing indifferent', to use a phrase that has emerged at different times in the Christian Church. Whether or not a minister wears a robe when he preaches, whether a church meets on a Friday or a Wednesday for its week-night Bible study or prayer meetings, whether a church has a blue or a red carpet, whether or not a layman has the ability or responsibility to pray in public, whether a person sits, stands or kneels when praying—these are things indifferent. Tithing is not like that.

Tithing was so deeply imbedded in the Jewish conscience, moreover, that it needed virtually no mention in the New Testament. Tithing was an assumption in Israel when Jesus came on the scene. 'Woe unto you, scribes and Pharisees, hypocrites! for ye pay tithe of mint and anise and cummin, and have omitted the weightier matters of the law, judgment, mercy, and faith: *these ought ye to have done, and not to leave the other undone*' (Matt. 23:23). It is striking that our Lord endorsed tithing in this verse. For He had little patience with the Scribes and Pharisees and wasted no time in getting to the heart of matters with them. Read Matthew 23 and you will see how our Lord pulled no punches with these men. He left no stone unturned. Even had He mentioned tithing in verse 23 and then let it alone it still would not have been a repudiation of it. But He went further; even though He called judgment, mercy and faith 'weightier matters of the law' and stressed these He did not leave it at that. 'These ought ye to have done, *and not to leave the other undone.*' Our Lord, I say, might have made light of their tithing 'of mint and anise and cummin,' or as the New International Version translates it: 'You give a tenth of your spices—mint, dill and cummin.' It would have been an apt place for Jesus to magnify such meticulous care to tithe—which He did—but also to leave it at that so we could see the humour, as it were, in His assessment of them. But He *took the care Himself* to sanction such bother to tithe, provided that it was done in the context of judgment, mercy and faith.

What the Pharisees had done was this. They upheld the Law of Moses which leaves no doubt on the matter of tithing. '*All* the tithe (NIV: 'a tithe of everything') . . . is the Lord's' (Lev. 27:30). Tithing was in fact the easiest part of the Law to keep. Not that tithing did not require self-discipline and care, but one could most certainly keep paying his tithes to the storehouse without having the slightest sense of judgment (or justice) to his fellow man, of mercy to his fellow man, or of personal faith. Paying a tithe on mint, dill and cummin could give the Pharisee a self-righteous feeling (not unlike that which a person might get by refusing to buy ice cream on Sunday). Jesus knew this. He attacked the Pharisees because of their distortion and lack of balance with respect to their understanding of religion. And yet Jesus honoured that part of the Law with respect to tithes! 'These (i.e., judgment, mercy, and faith) ought ye to have done, and not to leave the other (i.e., tithing) undone.' If tithing was a part of the Law that would or could be dropped under the New Covenant this is the place our Lord would have done it. He did not.

There are those who point out that Matthew 23:23 is the only place (other than its parallel passage in Luke 11:42) where our Lord endorsed tithing. This suggests to them that the New Testament presents a weak case for tithing. I might point out that our Lord only said 'Ye must be born again' to Nicodemus (John 3:1ff), but surely no one would seriously think that it is not a weighty truth because it emerged only with Nicodemus. If it is stated, 'But Jesus said, "Ye *must* be born again"'—and *must* is a strong term—I would point out that the same Greek word is used in John 3:7 as in Matthew 23:23: 'These *ought* ye to have done, and *not* to leave the other undone.' The Greek word *deo* (from which we get our word debt) means obligation or necessity, and the emphasis our Lord put on judgment, mercy and faith (or love—Luke 11:42) is not in the slightest diminished by the words, 'and not to leave the other undone'. Our Lord made no idle comments. His approval and exhortation to tithe ought to be sufficient motivation for any Christian who wants to be sure where he stands with regard to this subject.

If Jesus had not said, 'And not to leave the other undone' with respect to tithing·I wonder where missions would be today. That brief phrase (I suggest) has spelled the difference between success and failure in the enterprise of the Church of Jesus Christ at home and abroad. Where would foreign missions be without this verse? Had Jesus not made that statement there would probably be almost no motivation to give to God as we should. I repeat: if Jesus had not said it, it would not have meant a repudiation of tithing; but His saying it proves that tithing was not a part of the Law that was to be dropped (as if tithing had been a temporary principle).

All of us need encouragement with regard to giving. None of us by nature is a tither. All of us are congenitally allergic to tithing. We will look for every possible loophole by which we can justify our not tithing. Our Lord will not let us do that. As for missions, I wonder (humanly speaking again) where the Church would be today apart from Jesus' statement, 'Ye must be born again.' But He said it once and that was enough.

'But wait a minute,' says someone. 'The Apostle Paul did not mention tithing.' This at first would seem to be a weighty objection. But the same thing is often put forward regarding

Paul's doctrine of eternal punishment. Some have argued that it was Jesus who mentioned the vividness of eternal damnation in hell and that Paul was weak on this matter, if not silent. My answer: Jesus said enough about it so that Paul did not need to mention hell. When Paul did allude to it (cf. Rom. 5:9; 1 Thess. 1:10, 2 Thess. 1:9) it merely cohered with all Jesus said about it. God has ordered the New Testament to be written in such a manner that every word coheres with all the rest and that the succeeding books make a contribution. What Paul did say is enough to let us know what he believed about it, and I doubt not for a minute that in his personal preaching throughout Asia he left his hearers sobered with the awful news of the wrath to come. We have very little record of Paul's actual preaching, but we may be sure that his epistles as a whole represent the 'tip of the iceberg' of what he said when he was ministering in person. So with tithing. Paul was an articulate Jew who knew the Old Testament backwards and forwards. He did not have to spell it out by using the word 'tithe' any more than he needed to use the word 'hell' (which he never did in his epistles). I suspect Paul used the word *hell* in his preaching and I suspect he used the word *tithe* when building up the faith of the saints. I equally suspect his readers knew exactly what he meant by the phrase 'as God hath prospered him' in 1 Corinthians 16:2: 'Upon the first day of the week let every one of you lay by him in store, as God hath prospered him, that there be no gatherings when I come.' The phrase 'as God hath prospered him' (NIV: 'in keeping with his income') is about as clear a reference to tithing as one could get without actually using the word.

I hope that I have said enough to demonstrate already why every Christian should be a tither: it is Biblical. We shall of course return to this, but at this stage I would like to lay down three pragmatic reasons for tithing. The pragmatic test (by which I mean, does it work?) is *equally* Biblical. The Scriptural mandate should always come first, but the pragmatic test should follow. Some Christians are afraid of emphasising the pragmatic side. It is argued by some that if the Bible says it, that is enough. In other words, if it is Scriptural it does not matter whether or not it works. I am very sympathetic toward this line of reasoning. And yet I cannot ignore such verses as Malachi 3:10: 'Bring ye all the tithes into the storehouse, that there may be meat in mine house, and *prove me now herewith*, saith the Lord of hosts, if I will not open you the windows of heaven, and pour you out a blessing, that there shall not be room enough to receive it.' Or take the Apostle Paul's word in 2 Corinthians 9:6ff (where he is dealing explicitly with financial giving): 'He which soweth sparingly shall reap also sparingly; and he which soweth bountifully shall reap also bountifully. . . . And God is able to make all grace abound toward you; that ye, always having all sufficiency in all things, may abound to every good work'. The pragmatic test is not the most important but it is important enough that a lot in the Bible is said about it. These two verses alone are sufficient to encourage us to believe that our giving is followed by certain 'results'.

Three further reasons for tithing

1. *You should tithe because of what it will do for the work of God on earth.* Let us look at Malachi 3:10: 'Bring ye all the tithes into the storehouse, *that there may be meat in mine house.*' The same God who claims to own 'the cattle upon a thousand hills' (Ps. 50:10) and to whom the nations are but as 'a drop of a bucket' (Is. 40:15) equally claims His dependence upon His people to return to Him what is rightfully His—namely, the tithe. 'The tithe is the Lord's.' As a consequence the prophet Malachi regarded the withholding of *any* tithe as robbing God. 'Will a man rob God? Yet ye have robbed me. But ye say, Wherein have we robbed thee? In tithes and offerings.' Therefore 'bring ye *all* the tithes into the storehouse, that there may be meat in mine house.'

We are faced with an antinomy regarding tithing. An antinomy is two parallel principles that are irreconcilable but both true. It is a term that refers primarily to physics but it is equally true in theology. Dr J. I. Packer however tells us that, theologically speaking, the two parallel ideas only 'appear' to be irreconcilable. Dr Packer tells us this in his book *Evangelism and the Sovereignty of God*, in which he discusses the sovereignty of God and the importance of preaching the Gospel to all men. You also find an antinomy regarding the person of Jesus Christ: Jesus is God and man. He is not 50% God and 50% man but 100% God and 100% man. It is an antinomy. What then is the antinomy regarding tithing? Answer: *God owns everything but will have nothing unless His people give to Him*. In a word: God depends on us to tithe.

There is nothing more disgraceful than a church that struggles financially simply because its people will not tithe. There is nothing more melancholy than an underpaid minister. In most cases a minister is underpaid because the people in his congregation are not tithing. (In some cases a minister is underpaid because his deacons channel all excess income to everything else but the minister's financial needs. This is a separate discussion worthy of a book by itself.) There is not a church in the world today that should have any financial problem whatever if all its members would tithe. In most cases, were every member to tithe, the minister would not only receive his 'double honour' (1 Tim. 5:17) but the church would always have money to pay for its material needs. Not only that; the church could support missions with abundance, and never once would it need to have a bazaar, a jumble (rummage) sale, or any other incongruous means of raising money. The exception to this rule would be when a congregation most unwisely bites off more than it can chew in terms of church debt. Barring unwise use of funds I cannot conceive of a church having a financial problem of any serious consequence were all its members truly to tithe.

An example of what I am talking about is the Southern Baptist Convention. Southern Baptists, possibly more so than any movement in the world, are tithers. God has honoured Southern Baptists throughout the world and the reason is two-fold: an emphasis on missions and an emphasis on tithing. When it comes to the Great Commission (Matt. 28:19; Mark 16:15), we have before us a mandate which God takes very seriously indeed. God honours those who take it seriously and leaves us destitute of life and blessing if we don't. When it comes to the Great Commission you cannot out-do the Lord; when we *go* into the world preaching the Gospel to every creature we are dignifying His word and He blesses those who do in a most wonderful way. This in part explains the phenomenal success of the Southern Baptist Convention since its inception in 1845. But a great percentage of Southern Baptists are also tithers. Through the Cooperative Program there is support for the largest colleges in the world, the largest seminaries in the world, and the largest missionary organisation in the world. There are over 3,000 missionaries scattered around the globe. A theologically articulate friend of mine who had long been a champion of 'independent missions' once made a world tour of missions he had supported. He came back fully convinced that Southern Baptists had the best missionaries in the world. For one thing, he told me, they were the only missionaries he ran across that didn't have their hands out for more money—for every one of them were well paid by the Foreign Mission Board of the Southern Baptist Convention. The Foreign Mission Board is able to pay its missionaries well for one reason alone: so many Southern Baptists are tithers.

We won't be tithing in heaven. There will be no soul-winning in heaven. There will be no promise of blessing upon obedience in heaven. What we do for God we must do now. We can rest in heaven. We can learn in heaven. But we are not in heaven yet. Think what could be done for the Church of God in the world were every church member to begin to tithe right now. It would be wonderful. So much could be done.

> Only one life—'twill soon be past;
> Only what's done for Christ will last.

Were every member in your church to begin tithing next Sunday, I would predict that you could redecorate the church within six months; you could get all the necessary repairs fixed and paid for; you could pay your minister and all others on the staff with a sense of true dignity; you would not only have more money for missions but would have to elect a new committee to determine how to use the money coming in!

2. *You should tithe because of what it would do for God in heaven.* What on earth, you may ask, could tithing do for God? Answer: much. How so? Because He loves us so much. God has invested Himself in us. God gave us His Son. Those who dignify His Son's work on the cross have eternal life. Those who look to His Son are declared righteous. This is called justification by faith. But according to James not only is there such a thing as justification by faith but also justification by works. James was not contradicting the Apostle Paul. For James was not referring to the way we get to heaven when he said, 'Ye see then how that by works a man is justified, and not by faith only' (James 2:24). James was referring to quite a different use of the Greek word *dikaioo* (which simply means 'to make or render right or just'). That Abraham was justified by faith *alone* was acknowledged by James: 'And the scripture was fulfilled which saith, Abraham believed God, and it was *imputed* unto him for righteousness: and he was called the Friend of God' (James 2:23). What James was on to was with reference to the *obedience* of that person who *has been* declared righteous. There were two great watersheds in Abraham's life and James refers to both of them. The first great watershed is described in Genesis 15. God said: 'Look now toward heaven, and tell (count) the stars, if thou be able to number them: and he said unto him, So shall thy seed be. And he (Abraham) believed in the Lord; and he *counted* (that is, imputed) it to him for righteousness' (Gen. 15:5–6). That was when Abraham was justified by faith. This alone is what fits a man for heaven. Abraham became Paul's chief Old Testament example for the doctrine of justification by faith.

The second great watershed in Abraham's life was with reference to his obedience when God said: 'Take now thy son, thine only son Isaac, whom thou lovest, and get thee into the land of Moriah; and offer him there for a burnt offering upon one of the mountains which I will tell thee of' (Gen. 22:2). Abraham followed God's orders perfectly and fully intended to sacrifice Isaac. Abraham was unexpectedly prevented from following through this at the last second: 'Lay not thine hand upon the lad, neither do thou any thing unto him: for now I know that thou fearest God, seeing thou hast not withheld thy son, thine only son from me' (Gen. 22:12).

According to James, Abraham's *second* great watershed may be described in terms of justification by *works*. Abraham's sacrificing Isaac would not have helped him get to heaven because Abraham was going to heaven anyway; his trust in God in Genesis 15:6 assured that. But God wanted to see how much a man loved Him who was righteous by *imputation* (put to Abraham's account). Thus, according to James, what Abraham did in obeying God the second time was a *fulfilment* of justification by faith alone. Righteousness by imputation that is not followed by obedience is left unfulfilled, or incomplete. This does not mean that a man's justification is uncertain, or even rendered null and void by disobedience. But it most certainly makes him unfit to be called by God's name on earth. This is what James was after. James wanted to explain what he meant by the phrase 'justified by works' and therefore chose Abraham's obedience with reference to sacrificing Isaac as the clarification for what he meant by that phrase. 'Seest thou how faith wrought with his works, and by works was faith made perfect? And the scripture was *fulfilled* which saith, Abraham believed God, and it was imputed unto him for righteousness: and he was called the Friend of God' (James 2:22–23).

But there is more in this account of Abraham's obedience that will bear our attention. It is this phrase 'for *now I know* that thou fearest God, seeing thou hast not withheld thy son, thine only son from me.' Abraham's obedience obviously did something for God. 'Now I know you love me.' But did not God know Abraham's heart without Abraham having to go through this? Of course. God knows everything. 'All things

are naked and opened unto the eyes of him with whom we
have to do' (Heb. 4:13). Not only that; God knows everything
from the beginning (Is. 46:10). And yet here is this incredible
expression 'now I know'. Why is this there? Whatever
number of answers could be given, surely this much is
undoubted: God shared His feelings with Abraham. God let
Abraham know that He was pleased. Abraham's obedience
delighted God. Abraham's obedience did something for God.

This is a clue to every Christian that God really cares. God
cares about what we do. He cares about the way we live our
lives. And He cares whether or not we try to please Him.
When we *do* please Him it matters—so much so that He lets
us know. It is because He loves us so much.

In my own opinion James might have selected a different
episode in Abraham's life to demonstrate justification by
works, for Abraham's willingness to sacrifice Isaac was not
the only time (subsequent to his being justified by faith)
Abraham was obedient. Any obedience *after* being converted
may justly be called a righteousness by works. This is why
James later selected an entirely different person (Rahab the
harlot—James 2:25) to demonstrate the same truth. Any
obedience to the Lord is righteous; and to the extent that we
are first assured of our eternal salvation (so that works *don't*
contribute) such obedience may be called a righteousness, or
justification, by works. They fulfil, or fill out, our justification
by faith. Thus we are called the family of God's *friends*!

This then is why I have stated that tithing does something
for God. I believe this with all my heart. The way God says
'now I know you fear me' is by *blessing* us. How? So that 'there
shall not be room enough to receive it' (Mal. 3:10). Tithing
pleases Him because it is done in faith. Tithing, to repeat,
never comes naturally. Sometimes the struggle to begin
tithing may seem as painful as Abraham's struggle to give up
Isaac. We don't want to give up what is 'ours'. But if God
claims that the tithe is His we should not ask questions but
obey Him.

Abraham got Isaac back—'in a figure' (Heb. 11:19). That
means that Abraham came to grasp the profoundest of

truths, namely, that God's purpose in calling a people to Himself was to be at a spiritual level not the level of nature. And yet Abraham actually got Isaac back—and more. He was allowed to keep his son but, more than that, he saw God's greater purpose. This brings us to the third pragmatic reason every Christian should tithe.

3. *We should tithe because of what tithing does for us.* When God says 'now I know' there follows blessing upon blessing. So pleased was God with Abraham that God said: 'By myself have I sworn, saith the Lord, for because thou hast done this thing, and hast not withheld thy son, thine only son: that in blessing I will bless thee, and in multiplying I will multiply thy seed as the stars of the heaven, and as the sand which is upon the sea shore; and thy seed shall possess the gate of his enemies; and in thy seed shall all the nations of the earth be blessed; because thou hast obeyed my voice' (Gen. 22:16–18).

Whatever else may be learned from the story of Abraham and Isaac this much is clear: God blesses obedience. We literally cannot out-do the Lord. He waits to bless us. He wants to bless us far more than we want that blessing. But He waits to see whether we take Him seriously. To the man or woman who takes God seriously there is in heaven a 'now I know' response which results in blessing on earth such as we could not have anticipated. The blessing that follows obedience may be grasped both at a natural and spiritual level. When Abraham got Isaac back he got him 'in a figure'—showing the spiritual side of the blessing. And yet it *was* actually Isaac—in the flesh—showing this visible, or natural, side of the blessing.

What tithing does for us, then, is realised at two levels: the natural (or material) and the spiritual. The spiritual is by far the more important. For the very blessing that comes from heaven is essentially spiritual. It is God telling us He is pleased with us. How is this blessing known at a spiritual level? First, it does something for our very spirit—it 'looses', or releases, us. There is a deliverance that is felt within, an emancipation that cannot be got hold of any other way. There is a sense of freedom that had not been known.

A very interesting thing about freedom is that we often do not realise that we were in bondage until we get released. There are two kinds of bondage: that which we know about and that of which we are not aware. Many Christians are in bondage but don't know it. Many of us deny any sense of bondage. We get very defensive about the notion that we might be governed by a spirit of fear. We deny that we really do have a need. But when the release comes we find ourselves looking back on the condition from which we were just delivered with an almost staggering amazement. 'I can't believe I was in such bondage,' we say to ourselves. But it is only in the freedom from bondage that we see how bound we were all along.

Tithing is one way to find great spiritual release. Sooner or later we come face to face with this matter and the failure to walk in the light results in a greater bondage than ever. But when one enters upon the life of faithful tithing there is a sweet release to be experienced that cannot be fully explained to another person. This release by itself is enough to convince one fully how serious God is about this matter of tithing. The peace and joy are so wonderful that a frequent reaction is a kind of sorrow that one had not been doing it sooner.

The blessing at a natural level is inferior to the spiritual blessing I have described above. But it cannot be ignored. 'I will rebuke the devourer for your sakes, and he shall not destroy the fruits of your ground; neither shall your vine cast her fruit before the time in the field, saith the Lord of hosts' (Mal. 3:11). The 'blessing' promised by the prophet (Mal. 3:10) is primarily spiritual, but the fact that the prophet continues as he does indicates that this blessing is *not only* spiritual. God has a way of blessing us materially that just happens to coincide with our having become tithers. The 90% which we keep to ourselves after the tithe is given to the Lord has a way of equalling the 100% before the tithe. Sometimes the 90% goes far, far beyond what that 100%

would have purchased. How can this be? Frankly, I do not know. But I believe it.

In a previous pastorate I had a particular member who was (at best) a 'nominal' Christian. He came to church with his wife and children every Sunday morning but never at any other time. He put five dollars in the collection plate and felt that that was a bit too much but he reasoned that probably the church could use it. Besides, he concluded, he ought to contribute something to the service rather than only warm a church pew. But in a few months the preaching seemed to grip him. He came on a Sunday night! (In America when a church member begins going to church on Sunday evenings, something extraordinary is about to happen.) This man returned the following Sunday night. Soon he even became regular on Wednesday evenings (our mid-week prayer meeting and Bible study). But, lo and behold, he started to do something else—what he once vowed he'd never do: he began tithing. 'What I can't get over,' he confided to me after tithing for a few months, 'is that I haven't missed the money. In fact I think I might even have more than I ever had.' Today that man is a deacon and indeed a pillar in his local church. Another member in that same pastorate told me how he started tithing. He said that his former pastor in Detroit simply asked every member to tithe for three months, and then forget about it. 'We've been tithing ever since,' this man said. 'That was thirty years ago.'

2

THE ORIGIN OF TITHING

Tithing is not a twentieth century innovation, although there is some reason to believe that it has spread more widely in the last hundred years than in previous generations of the Christian Church. This to some provides a credible rationale for being suspicious of tithing. And yet it was precisely this latter mode of thinking that allowed some to reject the spread of missions in the nineteenth century, for William Carey lacked a concrete historical precedent for what he was doing.

God has used particular men and particular doctrines at various times in the history of the Church to bring to light what had gone unnoticed but which was solidly Biblical. The Deity of Jesus Christ was not a fourth-century innovation, but it seemed so to some. 'The world is against you,' they shouted at Athanasius. He retorted, flashing his black eyes, 'If the world is against Athanasius then Athanasius is against the world.' The doctrine of original sin was not a fifth-century innovation, but God used St Augustine to articulate a teaching that was so clearly in Scripture that it is astonishing that such should have lain dormant for nearly four centuries. The doctrines of justification by faith and assurance of salvation are not sixteenth-century innovations, but God used Martin Luther and John Calvin to restore to the Church such truths as turned the world upside down.

Tithing, however, was revived more as a practice than a doctrine in recent times, and the definitive statement on this subject has yet to be written. This practice has crossed denominational, geographical and theological lines. Bap-

tists, some proponents of the Wesleyan holiness movement
and certain Pentecostalists may largely have set the example
as the modern revivers of this Biblical truth. But in recent
years tithing has been taught and practised by Anglicans,
Lutherans and Presbyterians—not to mention others.

We may not know until we get to heaven precisely who the
first tither was, but apparently it was Abraham. Abraham
was Paul's example for justification by faith (an imputed
righteousness) but James' example for what he meant by
justification by works (actual obedience). It is striking that
Abraham should also be the chief example in the Bible for
tithing.

The first time the word *tithe* appears in the Bible is in
Genesis 14:20: 'he gave him tithes of all.' 'He (Abraham)
gave him (Melchizedek) tithes of all' ('a tenth of everything'—NIV). The story is this. Abraham's nephew Lot,
who foolishly had pitched his tent toward Sodom (Gen.
13:12), got caught in the cross-fire of a war between the king
of Sodom and other kings. Lot ended up losing both his
possessions and his freedom. Word of this got back to
Abraham who at once proceeded to rescue his nephew. The
success of Abraham (with 318 of his trained men) in defeating all the kings was phenomenal. Not only did Abraham
subdue the kings and plunder them but also rescued Lot in
the meantime, recovering all his goods 'together with the
women and the other people' (Gen. 14:16—NIV). At this
stage there emerges one of the more mysterious and sublime
events in all Holy Writ. Out of the blue, as it were, one called
'Melchizedek king of Salem and priest of the Most High
God', brought out bread and wine and blessed Abraham,
saying: 'Blessed be Abram by God Most High, Creator of
heaven and earth. And blessed be God Most High, who
delivered your enemies into your hand' (Gen. 14:19–20—
NIV). It is at this point that tithing comes into the picture.
'And he (Abraham) gave him (Melchizedek) tithes of all'
(Gen. 14:20).

There is no indication that Abraham was told to tithe by
Melchizedek himself. The Mosaic Law, moreover, which

later made tithing a legal obligation, actually came over four hundred years afterwards. Therefore Abraham was not keeping any prescribed command or law of God. Perhaps tithing did not begin with Abraham. This would not be surprising. Although Abraham was Paul's chief example for justification by faith, we know for a fact that Abraham was not the first man in the Bible to have faith (see Hebrews 11:4-7). For all we know Abel might have been the first tither. As for Abraham, however, we know that he was a pagan when God first reached him and there is not any proof that Abraham was conscious of continuing a godly tradition that preceded him. It would appear that God started all over, as it were, with Abraham. It would also seem that this is a reason the New Testament writers make so much use of Abraham.

A straightforward reading of Abraham's giving Melchizedek tithes suggests that this was done gratefully, voluntarily but also systematically. Abraham was extremely thankful to God. What a victory he had won! Not only had he rescued Lot, which apparently was the only thing he originally set out to do, but he plundered a number of kings to boot! Grateful Abraham was in a frame of mind to show gratitude. He was no doubt thankful to God. But how could he show it? There was no church, or temple or any such thing to which or through which Abraham could express his feelings of gratitude. The only godly tradition at hand was himself! But an outlet, as it were, by which Abraham could show his thankfulness did not appear until Melchizedek brought forth bread and wine.

Let us look at the account more carefully. 'Then Melchizedek king of Salem brought out bread and wine. He was priest of God Most High, and he blessed Abraham, saying, Blessed be Abram by God Most High, Creator of heaven and earth. And blessed be God Most High, who delivered your enemies into your hand' (Gen. 14:18-20—NIV). What moved Abraham to respond to Melchizedek as he did? How did Abraham know he could safely give tithes to a figure he had never met? One answer is that Melchizedek's *words* were apparently the first Abraham had heard other than from God Himself which resonated with all Abraham knew of the true God. This was no accident. Whoever Melchizedek was he most certainly appeared at the right moment—and articulated what Abraham felt.

As to what Melchizedek looked like, we do not know. As to whether Melchizedek's appearance affected Abraham (which is possible), we still do not know. As to whether Abraham perceived from the figure of Melchizedek what the writer of the Epistle to the Hebrews saw clearly is interesting but unprofitable speculation. All we know from the account in Genesis is what Melchizedek king of Salem *did* and *said*. What did Melchizedek do? He brought out bread and wine. That this prefigured both the death of Jesus Christ and the Lord's Supper I doubt not. What else did Melchizedek do? He blessed Abraham. But Abraham was already aware of being blessed, was he not? Indeed he was. But when Melchizedek blessed Abraham the latter *knew* that there was a direct connection between the victory he had just won and this figure who had brought out bread and wine.

What did Melchizedek say? He verbalised the blessing of Abraham. 'Blessed be Abram.' Melchizedek put into words what Abraham knew and felt. Furthermore, Melchizedek ascribed the cause of the blessing and victory to 'God Most High'. Abraham no doubt already knew this. But Melchizedek said it perfectly. Yet there was more. This Most High God was 'Creator of heaven and earth'. Whether Abraham had it put to him this way before, we do not know. But Abraham had no difficulty in believing in that. The God who had just accomplished the victory Abraham had witnessed could do anything. Believing in creation by God was an easy thing for one to accept who had already seen the transcendent power of God in his life. 'And blessed be God Most High.' Here was the first direct indication that God wanted the credit for all this. Here was the first hint that God wanted to be worshipped in the light of this victory. Here was the evidence to Abraham that God delights in man's gratitude. 'Who delivered your enemies into your hand.' God affirmed

Abraham in these lines by acknowledging that those he had plundered were enemies. Moreover, God affirmed Abraham in this victory. For God was behind Abraham—both in siding with him against the enemies but also in actually defeating the enemies. It was a subtle reminder that Abraham did what he did by the power of God, lest Abraham should be tempted to take himself too seriously later on.

What was Abraham's response to Melchizedek's words? 'Then Abram gave him a tenth of everything.' It was Melchizedek's words, then, that made the difference. 'It is the spirit that quickeneth,' said Jesus; 'the flesh profiteth nothing: the *words* that I speak unto you, they are spirit, and they are life' (John 6:63). The writer of the Epistle to the Hebrews tells us that Melchizedek was made 'like unto the Son of God' (Heb. 7:3). What Abraham saw and heard, then, was a *figure* of the Lord Jesus Christ. The word of Melchizedek therefore produced in Abraham a further gratitude toward God, for Melchizedek's word was a living word as from the Spirit of God. The response however was not only spiritual but material. Abraham gave a tenth of everything. It was not a tenth of his time. It was a tenth of the 'spoils', (Heb. 7:4) or 'plunder' (NIV).

There are some who think Abraham tithed not only from the spoils but also of what possessions he had already. Whether a 'tenth of everything' as it is put in Genesis 14:20 and Hebrews 7:2 means a tenth of all of what Abraham had accumulated before the battle with the kings is not clear by itself. Calvin seems to think that Abraham's tithes were 'taken out of his own property,' noting that Abraham returned everything which had been plundered from the king of Sodom (lest the latter say 'I made Abram rich'—Genesis 14:23). But I am satisfied that only the plunder from the battle with the kings is meant in the light of Hebrews 7:4. It is true that Zacchaeus was so overcome with gratitude that he said, 'Behold, Lord, the half of my goods I give to the poor; and if I have taken any thing from any man by false accusation, I restore him fourfold' (Luke 19:8). But Abraham's giving one tenth in the aftermath of the victory and in the light of having taken the spoils is consistent with all else the Bible has to say about tithes and 'increase' (Deut. 14:28). The tithe comes from the 'increase', or income. There is no warrant in the Bible that a new convert should turn over one tenth of all his worth to the Lord.

Abraham did what he did voluntarily. There was no Mosaic Law in force, then, neither is there any indication that Melchizedek came along and 'assessed' Abraham to the tune of 10% of the plunder. Melchizedek was not God's Inland Revenue agent. The government assesses—as does the Mosaic Law. But God puts those who have been touched by the Gospel on their honour. It does not however follow that God does not let us know what is pleasing to Him. For the truth is, He does let us know. But our response to the revelation is nonetheless voluntary.

Furthermore, there is not the slightest indication that Abraham was promised a blessing if he gave one tenth of all. He had already been blessed! There was not even the faintest suggestion in Abraham's response to Melchizedek that, if he gave a tenth he would be *more* blessed than ever. Abraham's motive was that of gratitude alone. His response not only prefigures the way the Christian should give but how the Christian should obey. For Abraham is also our example of the doctrine of sanctification. This was essentially James' point (James 2:21). The doctrine of sanctification does not teach us that we should be holy *in order that* our relationship with God would not be aborted. Our sanctification never gives us leverage with God. We plead nothing but the mercy of God through the atoning death of His dear Son. Sanctification is a response of gratitude. Holy living is a way of saying, 'Thank you, Lord, for saving my soul.' (That the absence of sanctification poses grave consequences for the backslider I will not go into here, only to point out that the friendship of the world 'is enmity with God'—James 4:4.) Salvation is by grace alone. Sanctification is our response to free grace. And yet sanctification pleases God. Not only that; it cannot be regarded as coincidental that God blesses obedience, as Abraham later learned (Gen. 22:12; James 2:23). But Abra-

ham was not thinking of further blessing when he paid tithes
to Melchizedek. It was a voluntary act of gratitude.

However, Abraham gave not only voluntarily but also
systematically. He gave one tenth of all. One tenth. The
tithe. That required some calculation. That required addition and subtraction. This meant taking care. It meant
looking over all that God had given and carefully working out
what one tenth was. It did not require a mathematical genius
to figure it out. Just a little addition and subtraction with the
care not to miss the slightest bit. It was not an estimate. It
was a tenth. When we 'estimate', we tend almost always to
set the figure in the direction we hope it will be (whether it is
the amount we hope we will earn, the size of a crowd or how
much we should give). Abraham's response to Melchizedek
was not an estimate. It was a tenth. Simple addition and
subtraction left no doubt.

One may say: 'But that is being legalistic.' That is one way
of looking at it. But there was no Law. Legalistic is a term we
tend to use if we object to the way things are being done. If it
comes to our employer paying us our salary, I doubt if we
would be very happy if he merely estimated our worth! When
it comes to giving God what is His we seem to become very
anxious not to be legalistic. Let us forget that word. Let us
call it being careful. Abraham was careful—careful enough
to give a 'tenth of everything'. That is our example. If we
follow Abraham's faith so that we may be called his children
(Gal. 3:29) and follow his obedience that we may be called
God's friends (James 2:23), let us follow his gratitude that we
may be cheerful givers (2 Cor. 9:7).

There is still more to be seen with regard to Abraham and
Melchizedek. As Abraham is our example, the one tenth of
the increase being the amount that should be given, the *object*
of Abraham's tithing also provides a lucid pattern for us. To
whom did Abraham pay tithes? Melchizedek. Who was
Melchizedek? He was a figure of Christ. He was 'like' the Son
of God. The writer of the Epistle to the Hebrews brought in
Melchizedek because of his discussion of the priesthood of
Christ. The writer claimed that Jesus Christ is our 'great

high priest' (Heb. 4:14). But the Law of Moses claimed that the priesthood should emerge from the tribe of Levi (Exodus 28) whereas Jesus obviously had descended from the tribe of Judah (Heb. 7:14). But Melchizedek, who came along over four hundred years *before* the Levitical priesthood was instituted, was actually called 'priest of God Most High' (Gen. 14:18), a fact no Hebrew (Christian or otherwise) would have disputed. For there it was – plainly stated in Genesis 14:18—Melchizedek was 'priest of God Most High'.

It was at this juncture that the writer of the Epistle to the Hebrews brought in Psalm 110:4: 'Thou art a priest for ever after the order of Melchizedek.' Psalm 110 was equally the word of God! The psalmist had made that declaration moreover long *after* the Mosaic Law had been brought in. The writer of the Epistle to the Hebrews thus argued that Psalm 110:4 could only have its fulfilment in the person of Jesus Christ.

When the Mosaic Law made tithing legal and binding upon Israel, it was the Levitical priesthood to whom tithes were to be paid. 'I give to the Levites all the tithes in Israel as their inheritance in return for the work they do while serving at the Tent of Meeting' (Numb. 18:21—NIV). Thus as Abraham had paid tithes to Melchizedek the priest, so Moses required tithes to be paid to Levi, for under the Law the priesthood emerged from Levi's posterity. Thus tithes were to be paid to support the work which the priests did in the tabernacle. In other words, tithes were to go for the service of God's work. The prophet Malachi would later apply the nickname 'storehouse' to this service (Mal. 3:10).

Thus Abraham's giving to Melchizedek prefigured the New Testament pattern, that those who preach the Gospel 'should receive their living from the gospel' (1 Cor. 9:14—NIV). The tithes would be the amount required to make this living not only possible but at a standard of 'double honour' (1 Tim. 5:17). Such dignity is not seen merely in terms of prestige but in the way that minister is paid. 'For the Scripture says, "Do not muzzle the ox while it is treading out the grain," and "The worker deserves his wages"' (1 Tim.

5:18—NIV). The tithes of all paid by all would enable every minister of the Gospel to live at this standard.

Tithes, therefore, should be solely and exclusively for the work of the Gospel. Tithes should not be given to 'charity', that is, any noble work. When a Christian gives his tithes, or any part of them, to non-Church organisations – no matter how valuable or useful to society they may be, that Christian robs the Church—and therefore God. Abraham's giving tithes to Melchizedek is enough to demonstrate this principle. It is precisely why Moses could later say, 'All the tithe of the land, whether of the seed of the land, or of the fruit of the tree is the Lord's: it is holy unto the Lord' (Lev. 27:30).

The tithe therefore should go directly and only into the storehouse—the ecclesiastical service of God. Charitable organisations should be sustained by either non-Christians or Christians who have first given *all* their tithes to the Church—and then to that organisation. That organisation moreover will be much, much better off and is far more likely to have God's blessing if it is not sustained by funds that belonged to the Lord. I do not doubt that a charitable organisation not connected to the Church can be blessed of God. This matter comes under the category of God's 'common' grace. But any organisation that receives funds that ought to have gone to the Church will be impoverished not enriched. If the Church got what it ought to have the whole world would be better off and worthy non-ecclesiastical organisations would be more blessed than ever. Funds that ought to be the Lord's which go elsewhere militate against God's blessing in the world generally and everybody loses.

Not only would tithes of all paid by all enable every minister to live at a standard of double honour but every congregation would have money to spend beyond its walls that would far exceed what the Church has been able to do at the present time. A short-circuit from the Christian to a non-Church enterprise will blow a fuse that affects God's blessing worldwide, but if every Christian will give all his tithes directly and only to the Church, everybody wins. The

Church is the salt of the earth (Matt. 5:13) and it ought to be the Church that provides the greatest stimulus to the world.

There remains yet one question that has been implicit all along in this discussion. How did Abraham know to give a tenth? Was it his own idea? If Melchizedek did not assess him for 10% of the spoil, what made him come up with that figure? Why not one twentieth? Or one fourth? Why a tenth? Was it a lucky guess? Did Moses legalise tithing because Abraham's example was as good as any?

We must be very careful in seeking to answer this question and not be too hasty to supply an answer. We do not know absolutely the answer to this question. We are on holy ground. It is not unlike when Moses, who kept glancing at the bush that was on fire, allowed curiosity to govern him. He proceeded to move up closer to get at the bottom of that extraordinary phenomenon—a bush on fire but left intact. 'Draw not nigh hither,' God's voice called out. 'Put off thy shoes from off thy feet, for the place whereon thou standest is holy ground' (Exod. 3:5).

The doctrine of revelation is holy ground. It is not a man-centred enterprise. What theology calls revelation, philosophy sometimes makes into epistemology—that is, pursuing 'to know how we know'. Epistemology however must stand back when revelation comes along, philosophy must remain subservient to Biblical theology. Revelation—that is, God's word being declared—is not up for grabs. The danger therefore in trying to get behind Abraham's decision to tithe, or to get into Abraham's mind, is that our desire to know becomes epistemological rather than theological and Biblical. In other words, we must be willing not to have it explained. But only believe.

I think however there are some relevant scriptures that might lead us to a happy and not-too-speculative understanding. The Apostle Paul spoke of the Gentiles who knew nothing of the Law but none the less have 'the work of the law written in their hearts, their conscience also bearing witness, and their thoughts the mean while accusing or else excusing one another' (Rom. 2:15). John said virtually the same thing

when he called the Lord Jesus Christ 'the true Light, which
lighteth every man that cometh into the world' (John 1:9). In
other words, the Law of God is already inherent in every man
by nature. The work of God in regeneration is not needed for
this to be true; it is already true. It is called *conscience*. Every
man has a conscience. Fallen man has a conscience. Unre-
generate men have a conscience. 'That which may be known
of God is manifest in them; for God hath shewed it unto them.
For the invisible things of him from the creation of the world
are clearly seen, being understood by the things that are
made, even his eternal power and Godhead; so that they are
without excuse' (Rom. 1:19–20). This is because man was
created in the image of God (Gen. 1: 26–27). The Fall of
man in Eden's garden did not eradicate the image of God but
left it severely defaced and marred. And yet the vestige of
God's image in man is sufficient to 'accuse or excuse'. This
vestige is the conscience.

Regeneration however leads the way to purge, or cleanse,
the conscience. 'How much more, then, will the blood of
Christ, who through the eternal Spirit offered himself un-
blemished to God, cleanse our consciences from acts that
lead to death, so that we may serve the living God!' (Heb.
9:14—NIV). Regeneration liberates the conscience to know
the will of God. 'For this is the covenant that I will make with
the house of Israel after those days, saith the Lord; I will put
my laws into their mind, and write them in their hearts: and I
will be to them a God, and they shall be to me a people' (Heb.
8:10). This was God's promise that the day would come
when His people would not need the external Law of Moses
to guide them; for the Law of God would be written on the
heart.

We must ever keep in mind that Abraham saw the Gospel
'in advance' (Gal. 3:8—NIV). I do not think it is too much to
say that Abraham was regenerated (born again) before the
New Testament doctrine of regeneration came along. For
that reason Abraham perceived the will of God long before
God verbalised it on tablets of stone. Thus Moses was not
only taking his cue from Abraham, or just sanctioning

Abraham, but was being governed by the same principle of revelation that affected Abraham in the first place.

And yet for all I know Abraham may have thought the one tenth was his own idea. This should not be surprising. For the Spirit of God has a way of working secretly in our hearts so that we cannot tell the difference between God's will and our own. The call to the ministry, for example, can be like that. One feels God's thumb in one's back, as it were, and wants to preach, or be a missionary, or full-time in Christian work or whatever with such zeal and ambition that the desire seems wholly natural. My own call to preach was so 'natural' that I delayed settling it for a long while because I feared that it was only my own idea. God often works like that. It may have been like that with Abraham.

But I do not believe that tithing was a lucky guess. I rather think that Abraham exemplified not only believing the Gospel in advance but also walking in the Spirit in advance. Thus the words of Melchizedek were not unlike the word of the Lord Himself—'spirit' and 'life' (John 6:63). Abraham walked in the Spirit long before the Law told us what righteousness was via the tables of stone. It is not surprising therefore that Paul could say, 'But if ye be led of the Spirit, ye are not under the law' (Gal. 5:18). For being led of the Spirit connects one to the same principle that governed Abraham before the Law came along. This is why Paul believed that the Holy Spirit alone is capable of leading one to godly living without the aid of the Law (Gal. 5:22ff).

And yet it does not follow that one does not need to be exhorted and encouraged by the word of God. God uses the word not only to engender life but also guidance. We need to hear the word. The Spirit works through the word—often by analogy. For what the life-giving word does is to 'trigger off' the silent voice in our regenerated conscience that was waiting to be heard. One scripture leads to another. One word will bring a person to see God's will in a matter which, on the surface, the same scripture might not have originally intended. This happens all the time through preaching. A person often becomes a Christian through a 'non-evangelistic' sermon. A person will often have a problem solved through a sermon that, on the surface, had no bearing on the situation at all. I was once preaching on James 1:22 ('Be ye doers of the word, and not hearers only') and uttered the words, 'Don't pray about it—do it.' A young man in the congregation felt God calling him into the ministry at that moment and is in the ministry of the Gospel today as a result.

I think we must therefore say that Abraham did what he did voluntarily and yet he had no choice. He did not have to tithe. And yet he did have to tithe. He had a choice. But he could not do anything else. Martin Luther had a choice but uttered that famous statement: 'Here I stand. I can do no other. God help me. Amen.'

This seems to be the way tithing originated. Nothing has really changed since.

3

THE GOSPEL AND THE LAW

A common objection to tithing is that it is bringing in the Law. Some say: 'We are not under the law but under grace' (Rom. 6:14), therefore tithing is 'out' insofar as the Christian is concerned. And yet those who take this particular line often state their view like this: tithing is only the beginning and we as Christians should give more than ever. Some people like this can be very vocal, insisting that any mention of tithing as such is legalistic. 'Should the Christian not be exhorted to give?' one will ask them. 'Oh yes,' the reply comes, 'the Christian should be encouraged to give but not the tithe for the Christian should go *beyond* the tithe.' It would seem that the preaching of tithing makes some people like this very upset, if not indignant. But they reply that in their view tithing as such is 'not on' because this puts a ceiling on our giving.

I am happy with the thought that we should not end with the tithe but should give beyond the tithe. Dr James Kennedy goes so far as to say that tithing is better 'the second time around'. By this he means that when some Christians begin to double-tithe, they are blessed more than ever. Who can object to the notion of giving beyond the tithe? Dr Kennedy insists that every Christian must *begin* with the tithe, however, and he most certainly is not among those who say that tithing is 'out' for the Christian. Quite the opposite. I asked him what the secret was with regard to the spectacular giving of the Coral Ridge Presbyterian Church in Fort Lauderdale, Florida, the fastest growing congregation in the United States at the present time. A membership of around

40 in the early 1960s has increased to about 5,000 in the early 1980s, and the value of their present property is over $10,000,000. It is well known that the church at Coral Ridge has grown largely owing to their evangelistic programme called 'Evangelism Explosion'. What is perhaps not so well known is that Dr Kennedy faithfully teaches and preaches *tithing*. His chief text is Malachi 3:10. His people have followed his leadership and have set an example for the whole world. One cannot but look at Coral Ridge with awe when it is considered what has been done by them under God. Part of the secret: tithing.

I have some reason to believe that many who object to tithing on theological grounds do so to camouflage their own practice. When I have been close enough to a person who takes this line, I sometimes have the impertinence to ask, 'Is your actual giving at the end of the year truly equal to or beyond 10% of your income?' Usually they will rub their chin or scratch their head or look down at the floor and admit in the end that they themselves give less than the tenth. Candidly, I have run into very few people who take this line whose actual giving even came up to the tithe.

There are some who object to tithing on the basis of legalism who will put it like this: we should give only as we feel 'led'. Their verse often is Galatians 5:18, 'If ye be led of the Spirit, ye are not under the law.' When I hear of people who give only as they feel 'led,' I think of the popular song 'Every time I feel the Spirit moving in my heart I'll pray.' I only ask: what if you *don't* feel led to pray, does it mean you should not pray? Candidly, most of my own praying is not carried out because I feel particularly 'led' to pray—as far as I can 'feel' it. I have to drive myself to my knees every morning, setting the alarm early enough to give sufficient time to pray, then call on God whether I 'feel' like it or not. Most often when the alarm goes off, I feel a certain resentment that I have to get up. Surely this is partly what Paul meant by being 'instant in season, out of season' (2 Tim. 4:2).

It is likewise stated by some that if you are tithing, you are not giving 'cheerfully'. This is of course a reference to Paul's words in 2 Corinthians 9:7: 'Every man according as he purposeth in his heart, so let him give; not grudgingly, or of necessity: for God loveth a cheerful giver.' Do people who take this line think that Paul would want you to bring the amount of your giving down to a level low enough for you to be able to give 'cheerfully'? The same would apply to the amount of time spent in prayer. The cheerfulness in giving should apply to the cheerfulness in prayer. And yet sometimes I do not feel 'cheerful' when I pray. Does this mean I should not pray? When I prefer to sleep instead of praying, should I sleep because I can do this more cheerfully? So when bills are pressing, should I abandon tithing for the moment because I cannot feel 'cheerful'?

The same principle applies to the command, 'Husbands, love your wives, even as Christ also loved the church, and gave himself for it' (Eph. 5:25). Why do you suppose Paul said that? Because sometimes we don't 'feel' love toward our wives as a spontaneous emotion. But we love them none the less. We love by showing. By doing. Not feeling. But doing. This is the theme that runs right through the New Testament. There are times we feel a certain emotion and this may be based upon our own mood or temperament or it may be based upon external circumstances. Other times we don't feel the same emotion. As for giving cheerfully, Paul added: 'And God is able to make all grace abound toward you; that ye, always having all sufficiency in all things, may abound to every good work' (2 Cor. 9:8). Why do you suppose Paul added those words? Because he wanted to *motivate* these Corinthians to give cheerfully. For giving cheerfully is *not* what comes very naturally and it frequently is *not* the way we are going to feel when a thousand and one needs compete for our pay slip. Sometimes I don't *feel* like praying but I know I should—so I do. Sometimes I don't *feel* love as an emotion for someone but I know I must do and act in such a way that *he* or *she* feels love from me! The result of doing what I ought to do—where praying, giving or disciplining my own feelings so that I demonstrate love – is that I am *so glad* I did what I knew I should do . . . Tithing is no different.

One of the more unsatisfactory expressions that has emerged in some quarters is that of a 'feeling' of being led by the Spirit. And yet I say this most guardedly because I too know the feeling of being led by the Spirit. I have it happening to me from time to time. But not all the time. In fact, not most of the time. For most of the time I do not get this feeling. What do I do then? I live by certain principles. These principles require an immense amount of self-discipline. When I am disciplining myself I do not feel 'led' to do this or that (or *not* do this or that) but I act as though it were totally and utterly in my own strength. And yet this very self-discipline is possible because of the hidden work of the Spirit. The Holy Spirit secretly lies behind my power of will although I may not be conscious of the Spirit's power at all. But it is the Spirit none the less who enables me to do what I do. The mistake one makes is to wait for the 'feeling'. Moreover, it is when I am living by principles of self-discipline that I really *am* pleasing to God—perhaps more than when I am being 'wafted' along by the Spirit. For I please God by faith alone not feeling.

There is perhaps no greater confusion among Christians than in their understanding of the place of the Law in the purpose of God. One cannot expect a very learned or complete treatment of the purpose and place of the Law in a book of this size, but an outline is in order. One hopes that enough will be said to achieve two things: 1. to heighten one's own assurance of salvation and 2. to heighten one's sense of discipline. If both should happen to the reader, an emancipating breakthrough indeed will have been achieved, and this is surely a matter of no small consequence.

What did Paul mean by these two remarkable statements: 'Ye are not under the law, but under grace' (Rom. 6:14) and 'If ye be led of the Spirit, ye are not under the law' (Gal. 5:18)? In both statements Paul meant freedom from the Law of Moses. The context of both demonstrates this. But does the absence of the Mosaic Law under the New Covenant mean 'no law' under the New Covenant? Did not Paul speak of being under 'Christ's law' (1 Cor. 9:21—NIV)? Did not

Paul speak of fulfilling the 'law of Christ' (Gal. 6:2)? Did not James speak of the Christian obligation to the 'royal law of scripture' (James 2:8)? These three verses point to the law of Christ's kingdom.

The word law is a translation of the Greek word *nomos* which, in turn, comes from the verb *nemo* which means 'to allot' and has the sense of 'what is proper'. In ancient times it came to embrace any kind of existing or accepted norm, order, custom, usage or tradition. The Law of Moses has been generally understood as having three aspects: Moral Law (Ten Commandments), Ceremonial Law (regulation of worship) and Civil Law (how people should govern themselves). The Mosaic Law was enforced through fear of punishment, as we shall see below.

The Law of Christ is what is proper to His Kingdom, namely, His rule in the lives of the people of God. It is summed up in what we popularly call the Golden Rule: 'Therefore all things whatsoever ye would that men should do to you, do ye even so to them: for this is the law and the prophets' (Matt. 7:12). Although it is called 'new' (John 13:34) it was nothing more than the summation of the 'spirit' of Moses' Law. Jesus called it loving one another as He Himself loved us (John 15:12). It is the way every Christian should strive to live.

The Law of Christ is higher than that of Moses. It sets a higher standard of righteousness, presupposes a different kind of motivation and is most certainly harder to keep. It requires a motivation and a discipline which Moses' Law knows nothing about.

Freedom from the Law of Moses is precisely what prepares one for the happy yoke of Christ's Lordship. Freedom 'from' is also freedom 'for'. 'Take my yoke upon you,' said Jesus, 'and ye shall find rest unto your souls. For my yoke is easy, and my burden is light' (Matt. 11:29–30). His commandments are not 'burdensome' (1 John 5:3—NIV), and yet to keep them is to demonstrate the very righteousness which the Law wanted to achieve (Rom. 8:3–4).

Many seem to think that the absence of the Law under the

New Covenant means an absence of self-discipline. And yet the truth is, it is not until we realise that we *are* emancipated from the Law of Moses that the Gospel of Christ gives true freedom for self-discipline. Under the Law of Moses there was no such thing as freedom of self-discipline. It was a case of 'Do—or else'. 'For it is written, Cursed is every one that continueth not in all things which are not written in the book of the law to do them' (Gal. 3:10). The Law produced the result one way: through fear. Through fear of punishment. There was the added promise of blessing upon obedience, yet even this was motivated by sheer fear. 'Behold I set before you this day a blessing and a curse; a blessing, if ye obey the commandments of the Lord your God, which I command you this day; and a curse, if ye will not obey the commandments of the Lord your God' (Deut. 11:26–28).

But under the New Covenant—the Gospel of Christ—we have the freedom of self-discipline precisely because our *faith*, not obedience, counts for righteousness (Rom. 4:3–5). In other words, when I know that I am saved by grace and not by works, I will need great discipline indeed to obey any of the commandments of Christ. For I realise that I am saved in the end, even if I fail to do all that I should, including tithing! I know that the New Testament requires transparent holiness of heart and life, that I love everybody, that I forgive my enemies, that I bless them that persecute me, that I pray for them that despitefully use me. But when God pronounces me 'free', then I'm free. My not forgiving my enemies poses grave consequences insofar as knowing the joy of the Lord (Rom. 14:17) and the Kingdom of God (Matt. 6:15). But nothing shall separate us from the love of Christ! 'If the Son shall make you free, ye shall be free indeed' (John 8:36). The Gospel is not a condition, 'Do—or else'. The Gospel is the good news that Jesus Christ saves!

Therefore precisely because I am free from the Law and because my failure to keep Christ's commandments does not invalidate my salvation, it requires great self-discipline indeed. If I am told that my obedience determines whether or not I am going to Heaven, I am not being motivated by love but by fear. But we have not received the spirit of bondage again to fear but rather 'the Spirit of adoption, whereby we cry, Abba, Father' (Rom. 8:15). 'For God hath not given us the spirit of fear; but of power, and of love, and of a sound mind' (2 Tim. 1:7).

What is our response to this Gospel? It is *love*. And yet this love is not necessarily a 'feeling'. It can certainly be that. Sometimes one is so overwhelmed that God should love us so much and trust us so much and grant us so much freedom that there is truly a spontaneous combustion of love. We all probably know this feeling very well. But love in the New Testament is seen essentially as a *voluntary* action. Love is an act of the will. It is something we *do* rather than feel. Love as a motivation is an act of self-discipline. One has to work at it.

To put it another way; sanctification is the response of gratitude but it does not follow that this response is always spontaneous combustion. It is usually a sacrifice. The writer of the Epistle to the Hebrews therefore spoke of the 'sacrifice of praise' and that doing good and sharing with others must be seen as no less than 'sacrifices' with which God is pleased (Heb. 13:15–16). This is why Paul said that those who believe in God should be 'careful to maintain good works' (Titus 3:8). Why be 'careful'? Because the easiest thing in the world is to lay aside good works because you know you *are* saved by grace. 'Let not sin therefore reign in your mortal body, that ye should obey it in the lusts thereof' (Rom. 6:12). Paul exhorted like this because we *are* saved by faith alone but also because obedience is *not* inevitable. We need to be reminded. Again and again.

> Prone to wander, Lord, I feel it,
> Prone to leave the God I love;
> Take my heart, O take and seal it,
> Seal it from Thy courts above.

Tithing is no different. We do not always feel like tithing. But we do it. Why? Precisely because we are 'not under the law but under grace' (Rom. 6:14). God has put us on our

honour. And yet when I think that God should do so much
for me, how can I but honour Him? In the words of C. T.
Studd: 'If Jesus Christ be God and died for me, then no
sacrifice can be too great for me to make for Him.'

In any case tithing did not come 'in' with Moses nor did it
go 'out' when the Law was fulfilled by our Lord Jesus Christ.
Tithing has always been 'in' where the Gospel is concerned.
This Gospel was given to Abraham 'in advance' (Gal.
3:8—NIV). Abraham's example of tithing was a pre-Mosaic
demonstration of what every believer should do in the light of
this Gospel. Thus when Paul exhorted the church at Corinth
that every Christian 'should set aside a sum of money *in
keeping with his income*, saving it up' (1 Cor. 16:2—NIV) he
showed that tithing was not abolished by the New Covenant.

When Jesus Christ came along He announced that His
purpose was to 'fulfil' the Law of Moses (Matt. 5:17). When
He uttered those words 'it is finished' (John 19:30), it was
one way of saying that He had fulfilled the Law of Moses.
This is why we refer to Jesus' death on the Cross as a 'finished
work'. All who believe in Jesus consequently are said to be
'in' Him. The phrase 'in Christ' is repeated over and over
again in the New Testament. This phrase means that those
who are in Christ are pronounced 'free' by the very Law that
had condemned us. Why? Because Christ fulfilled the Law
and we are in Him.

There are Christians who are unhappy because they have
not grasped this truth. This is why there is hardly anything
more important to understand in the Bible than the place of
the Law in God's scheme. If a person goes wrong on this he
will likely have a less than happy view of the very Gospel
itself. He is also likely to have an understanding of the
Christian life that engenders paralysis rather than freedom.

Tithing is not a 'carry over' from the Mosaic Law. It is a
'carry over' from Abraham. The Law is a parenthesis in
God's scheme. The Law was 'added' because of the sins of
Israel (Gal. 3:19), that is, it 'came alongside' (Greek: *para-
baseon*) (Rom. 5:20; Gal. 3:19), *until* 'the Seed to whom the
promise referred had come' (Gal. 3:19—NIV). The Law of

Moses had an historical beginning and also an historical *end*. 'Until.' This is why Paul could say that Christ is the '*end* of the law for righteousness to every one that believeth' (Rom. 10:4). Some Christians still fear the Law although they are 'in Christ'. Why? They are afraid that they must still answer for Moses' Law. The good news is that Christ kept the Law for us. When we see this, we will not be motivated by fear at all. We will then be in a position to accept the yoke of Christ gladly. It is a pity that some Christians struggle over this.

Abraham did not have this kind of problem. There is an obvious reason for this: the good news of his 'imputed' righteousness (that is, credited or declared) was not cut short by attached conditions. The Law of Moses was not around in any case. God merely said, 'Count the stars—if indeed you can count them . . . so shall your offspring be' (Gen. 15:5—NIV). Abraham had no reason to believe this promise (at the time he was not even a father and Sarah was growing old). But he did believe it! And his faith was 'credited to him as righteousness' (Gen. 15:6). Should someone think it strange that his justification by faith came in Genesis 15, when tithing was first done in Genesis 14 one need only read Genesis 12:1–4 to learn that Abraham was given and believed the same promise then. No one should imagine that Abraham became a tither before he believed the Gospel. Genesis 15 shows the promise to Abraham as being further established, as was his faith.

The Apostle Paul took up the argument, noting that there were no conditions attached to Abraham's salvation. 'Under what circumstances was it credited? Was it after he was circumcised, or before? It was not after, but before!' (Rom. 4:10—NIV). This was Paul's point when trying to recover the Gospel from legalism in the case of the Galatians. 'The Scripture foresaw that God would justify the Gentiles by faith, and announced the gospel in advance to Abraham' (Gal. 3:8—NIV). This was long before the Law came along. 'The Law, introduced 430 years later, does not set aside the covenant previously established by God and thus do away with the promise' (Gal. 3:17—NIV). For the covenant is fulfilled in Jesus Christ. For the promise to Abraham was to the 'seed'. 'The Scripture does not say "and to s̄ēds", meaning many people, but "and to your seed", meaning one person, who is Christ' (Gal. 3:16—NIV). Therefore if we are in Jesus Christ by faith, nothing can nullify the promise! This is why Jesus said: 'Abraham rejoiced to see my day: and he saw it, and was glad' (John 8:56).

We are not truly motivated to obey in love until we see that we have been accepted. God accepts us as we are, not as we should be. There is nothing so thrilling as knowing God really loves us as we are. This realisation is emancipating and paves the way to please God by voluntary obedience. This obedience, however, adds nothing to our being saved. We are saved by Christ's righteousness. The reason our obedience pleases God is because we demonstrate how much we appreciate Him for accepting us as we are. It pleases Him because He sees that *we* see that our obedience does not count for righteousness. 'So likewise ye, when ye shall have done all those things which are commanded you, say, We are unprofitable servants: we have done that which is our duty to do' (Luke 17:10). When God takes notice that *we* think that *our* righteousness *counts* for something, He regards it as 'filthy rags' (Is. 64:6). But when we do what we do as a way of saying 'Thank you', God delights in us. This is why Paul exhorted that we should give 'cheerfully'. When we give cheerfully, God not only delights in us, He shows it.

One way we show our gratitude to God is by tithing. Abraham was a tither. Why did he tithe? Because he, like all his true children, was 'not under law, but under grace' (Rom. 6:14). Away with the myth that tithing is bringing in the Law! Abraham was justified when there was no Law of Moses to guide him and he tithed when there was no Law to enforce it! 'Know ye therefore that they which are of faith, the same are the children of Abraham' (Gal. 3:7). It may be said, then, that there are two reasons why the Christian is not under the Law. 1. We are in the same position as Abraham who was declared righteous 430 years before the Law came along. 2. We are in Jesus Christ who fulfilled the Law for us

(Matt. 5:17). In other words, the Law has already been 'kept' by our Substitute—the Lord Jesus Christ.

Because Christ kept the Law for us we are in Him and *under* Him. He is Lord and Master. We take our orders from Him. Because Christ fulfilled the Law for us, then, we are said to be 'in' Him. But because He is not only our Saviour but also our Lord, we are 'under' Him. Paul called it being 'under Christ's law' (1. Cor. 9:21—NIV). I am 'in' Christ. I am 'under' Christ. In that I am 'in' Christ I know that the Law of Moses has been satisfied. In that I am 'under Christ's law' I know that I am to keep His own commandments. His commandments are summed up in one word: love. I am to strive for this, however much I fail. Keeping the law of Love would also mean keeping the very commandments of Moses, possibly without even realising it. This was Paul's point. Having said that 'he that loveth another hath fulfilled the law' (Rom. 13:8), the Apostle used some of the Ten Commandments as an illustration to prove that licentiousness is not possible. 'For this, Thou shalt not commit adultery, Thou shalt not kill, Thou shalt not steal, Thou shalt not bear false witness, Thou shalt not covet; and if there be any other commandment, it is briefly comprehended in this saying, namely, Thou shalt love thy neighbour as thyself' (Rom. 13:9). Consequently 'love is the fulfilling of the law' (Rom. 13:10).

But where does tithing come in with respect to the Law of Christ? Simply this: I am governed by God's word. The Law of Moses made tithing 'legal'. This in itself is a fairly strong hint how seriously God takes tithing. Murder was regarded as sin long before the Law came along (Gen. 4:7). Adultery was called sin long before the Law came along (Gen. 39:9). Tithing was practised by Abraham before the Law came along. But when the Law *did* come along, not only were murder and adultery declared a part of God's Law but Moses even declared that 'all the tithe . . . is the Lord's: it is holy unto the Lord' (Lev. 27:30). This is an undoubted demonstration of how important tithing was to God. 'That there may be meat in mine house' (Mal. 3:10).

God does not enforce tithing today. But to the person who is under Christ's Law there will be given—sooner or later—the light of tithing, God's way. When we are given the light of tithing, we show at that moment whether or not we submit to the yoke of Jesus Christ. 'His commandments are not burdensome' (1 John 5:3—NIV). Indeed, they pave the way for blessing beyond all we could have dreamed.

4

THE BLESSING OF TITHING

> There was a man,
>   Some called him mad;
> The more he gave,
>   The more he had.
>   John Bunyan

The Bible is full of promises of blessing upon the apparent condition of obedience. Note carefully that I say the 'apparent condition'. For any blessing from God is of grace and is filled with mystery. We cannot be exactly sure why God blesses us. In the end we are shut up to His own free grace.

The truth inherent in the above is also conversely true. God may withhold blessing from us and we cannot say exactly why. When God chastens us, it is not always traceable to any particular sin. After all, God has not dealt with us after our sins, nor rewarded us according to our iniquities (Ps. 103:10).

In other words, we must be guarded in ascribing the reasons for blessing and the withholding of blessing. We should not be hasty in making categorical assertions that will be impossible to prove. For example, it would be a mistake to hold out the promise that every tither will no longer have any financial problems. R. T. Williams (the man I was named after) related the account of a Christian businessman who became rather wealthy and gave liberally to the Church. A tragic turn of circumstances left him penniless. But when reflecting upon his turn of events this businessman observed that he had given no less than $100,000 to the Church, but added: 'Thank God, that is something that misfortune cannot wipe out. I still possess the $100,000 which I gave away.'

We must avoid the mistake made by Job's 'comforters', who could only think 'legalistically'. They were certain that Job's misfortune was due to some sin. The Jews always had difficulty in understanding the book of Job because they became entrenched in the notion that any illness, tragedy, financial reverse or whatever is negative was due to some sin. It followed for them that holiness and obedience always resulted in blessing and prosperity. The book of Job should be sufficient to make us guarded in our comments about God's blessing and His hiding His face. He may need no reason whatever—only His sovereign pleasure.

The Apostle Paul said: 'I know both how to be abased, and I know how to abound: everywhere and in all things I am instructed both to be full and to be hungry, both to abound and to suffer need' (Philip. 4:12). If this was true of Paul (no mean servant of Christ), we may safely assume that no amount of obedience—at any level—will guarantee smooth sailing all the time. The Lord loves 'whom he chastens' (Heb. 12:6), and His chastening must find some form. Whatever else chastening is, it almost always includes the hiding of God's face. When God hides His face, He gives no advance warning. He does not say: 'Next Tuesday afternoon at 2.15 you will notice that I have withdrawn the light of My countenance. Things will go wrong for you. You will be bewildered. But do not worry, it is only that I will be hiding My face from you.' No. God doesn't give us advance warning. He just does it. And He does it at the 'worst' possible time. It should not be surprising if God lets the matter of financial reverse, or insecurity, become the means of His chastening, even if we have been tithing. For often the essence of God's chastening consists in the fact that we do not know why He does what He does. It is true that sometimes we do know the reason. David did (2 Sam. 12:14). Jonah did (Jonah 2:9). But often God suddenly hides His face and allows a financial reverse to come and we don't know why. Yet we *do* know why. To test us—to see if we will serve Him, whether or not He blesses us. Job said, 'the Lord gave, and the Lord hath taken away; blessed be the name of the Lord' (Job. 1:21).

The promises of blessing in the Bible are often set in the language of accommodation. God stoops to our level to encourage us. He reaches us where we are. 'He knoweth our frame; he remembereth that we are dust' (Ps. 103:14). To encourage us, God accommodates us at a level that will motivate us. This is partly why Paul could tell us to give 'cheerfully'. After all, he went on, 'God is able to make all grace abound toward you; that ye, always having all sufficiency in all things, may abound to every good work' (2 Cor. 9:8). Not only that; this exhortation to become a cheerful giver followed these words: 'He which soweth sparingly shall reap also sparingly; and he which soweth bountifully shall reap also bountifully' (2 Cor. 9:6). These words are clear enough and their implications are obvious.

Are these idle promises? They are not. They are not only absolutely true but have been proven again and again by a vast company of believers.

But are these promises absolute guarantees that the cheerful giver will never have a financial reverse? No. Why not? Because God hides His face to test our motives. It was said of Hezekiah, 'God left him to test him and to know everything that was in his heart' (2 Chron. 32:31—NIV). God reserves the right at any stage in our Christian pilgrimage to answer the question: 'Doth Job fear God for nought?' (Job 1:9).

We therefore would do ourselves an immense favour to check out our motives for tithing right from the beginning. For the danger in this very chapter is that one will be motivated to tithe for the wrong reason. Even this could result in someone becoming prosperous (for God honours His word), but I would not want to encourage anyone to become a tither for the wrong reason.

Behind Paul's exhortation to us to be cheerful givers lies not only the promise of blessing but also a protection against bitterness should God withhold blessing. If we give cheerfully, we will be built up in the faith to the extent that we give because it is *right*, not because it pays. We give cheerfully because 'God is able', not because of an absolute promise to prosper us. Giving cheerfully is to affirm God's power and glory. Giving cheerfully, then, is to show a godly concern. A godly concern envisages the greater glory of God, therefore the absence of the blessing will not result in bitterness. This is what is lovely about the testimony of the aforementioned businessman: 'Thank God, that is something that misfortune cannot wipe out. I still possess the $100,000 which I gave away.'

The tither should possess the 'but if not' faith. It was the faith of Shadrach, Meshach and Abednego who refused to bow down before King Nebuchadnezzar's golden image. They risked being thrown into the fiery furnace. They said: 'Our God whom we serve is able to deliver us from the burning fiery furnace, and he will deliver us out of thine hand, O king. *But if not*, be it known unto thee, O king, that we will not serve thy gods, nor worship the golden image which thou hast set up' (Daniel 3:16–18). The tither's faith must be exactly like that. Our God is able to bless us, even make us prosper abundantly because we take Him at His word. But if He doesn't, we still know that 'God is able'. In the meantime we will tithe anyway! That is cheerful giving.

We cannot be too careful about this principle. A godly concern must lie behind our tithing or we could set ourselves up for a very keen disappointment. Once I received the following letter: 'Last week I received a crippling tax demand that just happens to equal my yearly tithe. It is payable within one month or a 12% interest starts to accrue . . . if I am in need, shouldn't I stop tithing?' This person wondered if 'we should leave out the expecting-God-to-bless part?' My answer is, No. To both questions. Why should we ignore the plain promises of God's infallible word? He is the one who put those promises there, not us! We should quote them and appeal to them again and again. But with the knowledge of His glory. It is His own prerogative to hide His face from us and He frequently chooses the matter of economy as the only instrument that will effectively drive us to our knees.

God hides His face only for a season. I suggest that if He hides His face from us by putting us through economic difficulty—even though we have been tithing—it is to test us to see whether or not we will continue to do exactly as His word tells us, to give God what is *His*. In my files I have stories like this: 'The first week I started tithing my car broke down and it cost me five times my tithe.' 'The first week I started tithing I ended up in hospital.' 'I was tithing regularly for three months and I got laid off work.'

There is an American expression: 'Don't tell the score in the middle of the ball game.' That is what the above testimonies did. One can be equally foolish in the opposite way, moreover. I heard an American dentist give his testimony that the very week he started tithing over $1800 of overdue fees came in from patients. That is *not* what God has in mind. It is the long run that matters. The kind of testimony I have in mind is one that was put like this: 'I have been tithing for years. We've had ups and downs. But God has supplied every need. God has always made the 90% go further than when we used to keep the 100% to ourselves.' It is the long run that counts. 'I will never leave thee, nor forsake thee' (Heb. 13:5).

There are some Biblical texts concerning giving and being blessed that will bear our looking into. Perhaps the most outstanding one is Malachi 3:10. Some may object to this verse because it comes within the parenthetical period of the Law. I answer: most of the Old Testament does. Does that mean we ignore it? We would have to omit the psalms as well. What if God wanted to motivate His people during the period of the Law? There would only be one reason for doing so, and that is because He loved them so much. That the Apostle Paul should use virtually the same language in 2 Corinthians 9:6–8 is sufficient to box any of us in to see the spiritual continuity between the promise of Malachi and that of Paul. Though Israel was under the Law at the time Malachi's promise came along, do not forget that it was the same God, our God, who gave it!

Malachi 3:10 reads: 'Bring the whole tithe into the storehouse, that there may be food in my house. Test me in this,' says the Lord Almighty, 'and see if I will not throw open the floodgates of heaven and pour out so much blessing that you will not have room enough for it' (NIV). This command and promise is set in the context of a severe warning to the children of Israel. 'Will a man rob God? Yet ye have robbed me. But ye say, Wherein have we robbed thee? In tithes and offerings.' The reason withholding tithes may be said to be robbing God ought to be fairly obvious to the reader by now. 'The tithe . . . is the Lord's' (Lev. 27:30). What Abraham had given to Melchizedek turns out to be nothing more than what was actually God's all along!

In other words, the tithe is already the Lord's. He claims the 10% of the increase or income from the start. It is not a question whether or not God should have it; it *is* His—already. He says so. But the remarkable thing is, He puts us on our honour to turn it over to Him.

The same principle lies behind Paul's words: 'For ye are bought with a price' (1 Cor. 6:20). In other words, these Corinthian Christians were told by Paul that their bodies were already God's—not merely by creation but by redemption, the price being the blood of God's own Son. Thus these Corinthians were already God's. They were not their own. And yet Paul went on to say to them: 'Therefore glorify God in your body, and in your spirit, which are God's' (1. Cor. 6:20). If they did not glorify God in this manner, they risked two things: 1. the loss of their reward in Heaven (1. Cor. 3:15), and 2. their very lives. 'If any man defile the temple of God, him shall God destroy; for the temple of God is holy, which temple ye are' (1 Cor. 3:17). Paul took note that among these very Corinthians were many who were weak and sick, 'and a number of you have fallen asleep' (1 Cor. 11:30—NIV). In other words, God took them right on home prematurely, as it were, because they had not kept faith with God's right to their bodies.

Tithing, although obeying a commandment at a different level, is no different in God's sight. As the body is the Lord's, so the tithe is the Lord's. To abuse the body is to abuse the temple of the Holy Spirit, so also is the withholding of God's tithe to rob Him of what is His own. He puts us on our honour to obey Him. Not to do so is to our spiritual impoverishment, perhaps even our peril. For Malachi continued: 'Ye are cursed with a curse: for ye have robbed me, even this whole nation' (Mal. 3:9). It would seem from this that the people of God in Malachi's day found other uses for their money. Perhaps they couldn't 'afford' to tithe. Perhaps they thought the tithe really didn't matter all that much. 'But,' says Malachi, 'look around. Haven't you noticed? You are cursed with a curse. You are in trouble as a nation. The reason is that you have literally robbed God!'

Malachi's message is most fitting and relevant (but no less unpleasant) today. Every nation under the sun today seems to be in financial difficulty. An unbalanced budget, rising inflation, low cash flow, high unemployment, bewilderment. We could go on and on. The story is familiar and commonplace. I say it again: the root of the problem is the failure of the professing people of God to tithe. While a nation totters on the brink of being demoralised the Church offers no leadership. The failure to tithe is no doubt only one symptom of a deeper malady, and yet I doubt not that at our fingertips is an opportunity to reverse the trend. If *all* of the people of God would begin *now* to give their tithes to God's storehouse, two things would happen. 1. The Church would come alive and morale would be restored both to the ministry and to the Church membership. 2. Credibility would be restored to the Church, therefore the world (including government) would take the Church seriously. If these two things only came into play a third factor of no small importance would be in operation: God's own blessing. 'Righteousness exalteth a nation: but sin is a reproach to any people' (Prov. 14:34). For when the Church is faithful to its trust, God moves in to bless both it and all which it touches. God does it. He has a way of restoring normality, even prosperity, right out of the blue. It is that which defies a natural explanation. But that is the way God works. When the Church is rebellious and disobedient, that nation will be in awful difficulty. Government can bring in the finest minds, the most brilliant economists, the most able statisticians. But bewilderment and confusion pervades the atmosphere. But let the Church get right with God and all the world is affected by it. Tithing is but a beginning. But a most solid beginning. It is within the grasp of God's people to do something about this matter—right now.

What is the solution? Malachi 3:10: 'Bring ye *all* the tithes into the storehouse, that there may be meat in mine house.' In the case of Israel at that particular time, the tithes totalled more than a mere 10%. For under the Law there was an elaborate system of tithes and offerings. There was more than the basic tithe, for there were 'tithes'. There was 1. the tithe for the support of the Levites (Num. 18:20–32; Lev. 27:30 –32); 2. the second tithe, or the festival tithe, to provide the travel and food costs of the worshippers attending the major Jewish feasts (Deut. 12:5–19; 14:22–27); and 3. the charity tithe, given every three years and used for the care of the poor. It may be reckoned that these Jews gave at least 23½% of their income.

Are Christians bound to tithe like this today? No. This elaborate system was a part of the Mosaic Law and it is at this point we may see a noticeable difference between the Law and Christian freedom. One cannot help but notice that the Christian at this point has a 'lower' standard. Whereas I said earlier that the Law of Christ is a higher and more difficult law to keep, at this point such would not be the case. I am satisfied that the Christian obligation is a basic 10% of his income. To those who can double-tithe, well and good. Indeed, there is the reference in Malachi 3:8 to tithes 'and offerings'. There is the tithe. There is that which is beyond the tithe. 'Offerings' surely point to collections taken for specific needs beyond the ordinary requirements for the regular functioning of the work of God. Every Christian must be prepared to give offerings above his tithe from time to time. But that it should come up to 23% or more is another matter. In some cases it will, in others it will not. Some can give more than others.

I am sure of this. If every member of the Christian Church

will only begin *now* to give 10% of his annual income—even if
this should be the maximum, one can safely predict that
'there will be meat' in God's house.

The 'storehouse' is a nickname for the Temple of God, or
any local synagogue or assembly. It was where the tithe,
having been laid aside for a period of time, could finally be
'deposited'. Paul no doubt had this very practice in mind.
'Upon the first day of the week let every one of you lay by him
in store, as God hath prospered him' ('set aside a sum of
money in keeping with his income, saving it up'—NIV) (1
Cor. 16:2). The storehouse was the repository, the treasury.
Not to bring the tithes to the house of the treasury was to trifle
with God. In other words, the Hebrews were not to 'sacrifice'
their tithes, as if the money was to be consumed. Had there
been such a thing as paper money, they were not to strike fire
to this money. This was actual money, currency, to be used,
spent, by those who were entrusted with the work of God.
They were to bring the money—not money to be consumed
but money that was *needed*.

Why? Because God needed the money! It is a way of
saying, 'He has no hands but our hands.' The 10% of the
people's income was to be deposited in the Church treasury,
'that there may be meat in mine house.' The work of God
takes money. It costs to advance the message and mission of
the Most High God. He has cattle on a thousand hills, yes,
and all the earth and its fulness belongs to God. But it
happens that God has turned His work over to men. He did
this by choice. 'It pleased God by the foolishness of preaching
to save them that believe' (1 Cor. 1:21). 'Don't you know that
those who work in the temple get their food from the temple,
and those who serve at the altar share in what is offered on
the altar? In the same way, the Lord has commanded that
those who preach the gospel should receive their living from
the gospel' (1 Cor. 9:13–14—NIV). This passage serves
virtually as Paul's own commentary on Malachi 3:10. 'That
there may be meat in mine house.'

This, then, is the chief motive for tithing. 'That there may
be meat in mine house.' The chief motive for tithing is not the

blessing that we will get from obedience. The chief motive is
that we are jealous for God's work, that we want it to thrive
and prosper, that there be no hindrance whatever owing to
lack of funds. We give because we care. We give because we
believe the Gospel. We give because we know God has used
men to advance His work. Tithing is God's way.

What is sadder than a church building that is run down?
What is sadder than a minister of the Gospel who can hardly
pay his bills? What is sadder than shabby-looking church
premises? What is sadder than the general feeling of financial
oppression insofar as the Church is concerned? All this can
only be true because the people of God have robbed God of
what is His. It is not only disgraceful, it is sad. All of us must
hang our heads in shame when we consider the state of the
Church at the present time in most places. Tithing is one way
of rectifying this. There are other ways of course, but tithing
is one way in the meantime.

Why should you be a tither? That there may be meat in
God's house. Why should you be a tither? Because you care.
Because you are jealous for the work of God. If nobody else in
your congregation is a tither, you must begin tithing *now*
because you care about your own relationship with God. It is
He who sees what you do. That matters. There is no better
reason for tithing than that.

At this stage Malachi makes one of the most extraordinary
claims in all Holy Writ. What follows is to me one of the most
remarkable lines I know about. Here follows the *only place* in
the Bible we are told to prove God. 'Prove me now herewith,
saith the Lord of hosts.' This is extraordinary. There is no
other place in the word of God that suggests proving God.
The Bible in fact makes no attempt to prove God. It only
begins: 'In the beginning God' (Gen. 1:1). There is an aspect
of theology called apologetics. It deals with the defence of the
Christian faith and of the Bible. Many great theologians were
basically apologists, like Thomas Aquinas. Aquinas spent
years developing the various proofs of God, as the 'cosmolo-
gical' proof of God. He reasoned that you could prove God
from nature. Some theologians have made other efforts.

Anselm developed what is called the 'ontological' proof of God, that one conceives in one's mind a being 'than which no greater can be conceived'—namely, God. We could mention others.

But here is apologetics at its finest. Malachi's apologetics. 'Prove me now herewith.' Do you want to prove that God exists? Do you want to prove that God is alive and well? Do you want to prove that God still does things? Honour Him with your substance and you will see Him work in a manner that will exceed your greatest expectations. 'Prove me now herewith, saith the Lord of hosts, if I will not open you the windows of heaven, and pour you out a blessing, that there shall not be room enough to receive it.' As A. W. Pink put it: 'I tell you, my friends, my soul is overwhelmed by the amazing condescension of the Most High to place Himself in such a position. God allows Himself to be placed on trial by us, and tithing is a process of proof. Tithing is a means whereby we can demonstrate in the material realm the existence of God and the fact of His governorship over all temporary affairs.'

God didn't have to add that. He had the right simply to rebuke these Jews for not giving Him what is His. He could have ended the discussion with that reference to the 'curse'. But he didn't. In singular kindness and tenderness He stooped to motivate us. He condescended and put His own reputation on the line. This is why there are innumerable testimonies as to the blessing people have received from tithing. God honours obedience.

The apparent condition for such blessing is obedience. Note: it is not an absolute promise. Notice how Malachi put it. 'Prove me . . . *if I will not* open you the windows of heaven.' 'Test me in this . . . and *see if I will not* throw open the floodgates of heaven' (NIV). In other words, God challenges us. And yet He has put it in such a way that He is free to bless or withhold blessing. As Paul put it, 'God is able'. There was no absolute guarantee. No, not absolute. But it comes awfully close. So close that, candidly, I doubt if there has ever been a living person who regretted a lifetime or long period of tithing. Most would be tempted to say that their relative comforts of life and their faithful tithing are inseparably connected. For it is God Himself who encourages us to think like this.

What is it that God suggests will follow our tithing? That He will open the windows of heaven. 'See if I will not throw open the floodgates of heaven and pour out so much blessing that you will not have room enough for it' (NIV). Were we to stop right there, we might limit the blessing to the spiritual realm. If that were true, I would be very happy indeed. For I should prefer God's own spiritual blessing a thousand times over to any material benefit. If tithing alone were to provide blessing like that, how can we keep from tithing? And yet it is true that, once a person comes upon the light of tithing he must go one of two ways: forwards or backwards. If one draws back from tithing, once one has been exposed to it, I predict that the light in the soul will become dim, if not very dark indeed. But should one walk in this light, the primary result will be spiritual release from within. You will feel not only 'good' inside but will notice a new sense of freedom, a new glow in living the Christian life, a renewed appreciation of studying God's word, and you'll be easier to live with! I promise it.

But Malachi appears to mean more than a spiritual blessing. 'I will prevent pests from devouring your crops, and the vines in your fields will not cast their fruit, says the Lord Almighty' (Mal. 3:11—NIV). This is a clear indication of prosperity not merely at a spiritual level but at a material level. What were crops or fruit to these Hebrews living in Malachi's day would be something else today—sales to the salesman, business to the businessman, clear thinking to the man who uses his mind, 'good breaks' to the investor, happy harvest to the farmer, open doors to the one who must expand, the rise in pay for the clerk, secretary, nurse, policeman, lorry driver, factory worker, or the mere absence of trouble. There can be no doubt that Malachi encourages us to believe that if we truly give God what is His by honouring Him with our substance, He will in turn do things for us that can be visibly seen and felt at a material or natural level. 'I will rebuke the destroyer for your sakes' (Mal. 3:11). That is God's own promise.

This word of promise is not exclusive to Malachi, as we have seen. The Apostle Paul takes up the same line. The Bible in fact is full of similar promises. 'Honour the Lord with thy substance, and with the first-fruits of all thine increase: so shall thy barns be filled with plenty, and thy presses shall burst out with new wine' (Prov. 3:9–10). 'Give, and it will be given to you. A good measure, pressed down, shaken together and running over, will be poured into your lap. For with the measure you use, it will be measured to you' (Luke 6:38—NIV). 'One man gives freely, yet gains even more; another withholds unduly, but comes to poverty' (Prov. 11:24—NIV). As John Bunyan summed it up:

> There was a man,
> Some called him mad;
> The more he gave,
> The more he had.

'A generous man will prosper; he who refreshes others will himself be refreshed' (Prov. 11:25—NIV). 'Remember this: Whoever sows sparingly will also reap sparingly, and whoever sows generously will also reap generously' (2 Cor. 9:6—NIV). It is hardly surprising, then, that our Lord should put His own endorsement upon the faithful practice of tithing. It was an affirmation of Abraham, Jacob, Moses and Malachi in one line: 'these ye ought to have done, and not to leave the other undone' (Matt. 23:23).

Tithing is in fact a Christian duty. It really comes under our Lord's summation in Luke 17:10: 'So likewise ye, when ye shall have done all those things which are commanded you, say, We are unprofitable servants: we have done that which was our duty to do' ('We are unworthy servants; we have only done our duty'—NIV). And yet God delights in showing us that He is pleased with us. It is as though He cannot keep from concealing His own pleasure with us. So

what does He do? He shows it. He has shown it for so long
and so often and to so many that nobody knows who said it
first: you cannot out-give the Lord.

5

DO YOU HAVE ANY QUESTIONS?

At our Friday evening Bible study I leave time for questions. We have microphones stationed in the aisles so that everybody can be heard. We have had some very fruitful evenings. Almost always the questions that have been raised were in several others' minds. Questions serve to clarify issues that have been raised, and often a breakthrough comes at the most unexpected time. Sometimes a breakthrough takes place when what seems to be a small matter is faced.

I'm sure the reader has had at least one or two questions come to mind, and if all the readers had the opportunity to ask a question at this stage, I'm sure I would have to write a book many times this size! What I shall do in this closing chapter is to anticipate questions the reader might well have. I have envisaged these questions following my own pastoral experience. I fear that I shall no doubt leave out questions I will think of after this book emerges from the press.

1. *Should we tithe the 'gross' or the 'net'?* This is often the first question one thinks to ask when one begins to be persuaded of the Biblical principle of tithing. I answer, the Lord's tithe is 10% of our gross salary or wages, or 10% of our net gain if we are in business for ourselves.

It must be remembered that what is deducted from our gross pay is for our own good. We in fact get it back, including what is provided by our income taxes. In Britain we have our health insurance deducted, consequently our medical fees, hospital costs and other expenses are actually benefits due to our income. If a person tithes only the 'net', i.e. 10% of his actual pay packet, he is forgetting that the deductions ultimately are his as well.

I would caution the reader that to narrow the basis of the tithe to the 'net' is to undermine the promise of God's blessing. For to tithe only the 'net' borders on giving grudgingly and may well militate against the promise of blessing. It is as though one does not really believe one cannot out-give the Lord. Furthermore, once a person begins to think of 'gross' and 'net' and opts for the latter, he will find himself thinking of other items that, though not deducted by his employer, he himself will deduct from God. I have heard of some people who deduct their transportation costs to church, of others who deduct any unforeseen expenditure that they feel God would approve of! When we begin to think like this, do not be surprised in the end if God gets nothing at all. The person in business for himself must be particularly aware of this pitfall.

Remember: God puts us on our honour to give Him what is His. Jack Taylor put it like this: 'I see the tithe as that which we turn over to God; essentially, in the strictest sense, it is not giving. It is turning over to God that which is already His.' Manley Beasley made this observation: 'My own personal experience in giving has been that I cannot out-give God. Every time I have taken on a project of giving, God has taken on the project of giving back. I can honestly make the statement, even after more than thirty years.'

When we look at the matter in the light of God's power and grace, it is not likely we will ever be very tempted to tithe only the 'net' again.

2. *Why should I tithe when my actual tithe is so small?* You should do it because it is right. The amount is utterly irrelevant. Donald Grey Barnhouse used this illustration: 'Let us think of each man in terms of capacity. The great and gifted leaders who may be described in terms of thousand-gallon capacity are few and far between. There are more who have a hundred-gallon capacity; still more with ten and five-gallon

capacity; multitudes with one-gallon capacity, and vast multitudes that must be measured in terms of quart, pint or even ounce capacity. Judged by worldly standards, those with great capacities seem to have all the breaks. Honour comes their way. They are seen, known, praised and rewarded. They own a larger portion of the world's goods. A thousand-gallon tank that is half-full appears infinitely superior to the half-pint jar that is overflowing. But, as God sees them they may have great lack. If the Bible teaches anything, it is that God is more delighted by the overflowing half-pint than He is by the thousand-gallon tank, half-full of its own doings. When any person becomes enamoured of his own capacity, he becomes useless to God.'

The story of the 'widow's mite' comes to mind. 'Jesus sat down opposite the place where the offerings were put and watched the crowd putting their money into the temple treasury. Many rich people threw in large amounts. But a poor widow came and put in two very small copper coins, worth only a fraction of a penny. Calling his disciples to him, Jesus said, "I tell you the truth, this poor widow has put more into the treasury than all the others. They all gave out of their wealth; but she, out of her poverty, put in everything—all she had to live on"' (Mark 12:41–44—NIV).

God sees the heart. That makes all the difference, not the actual amount. In any case, the tithe is still the Lord's.

3. *Is the 'storehouse' always the Church?* In my view—yes. I do not think that many Bible scholars would differ on the point that the New Testament ministry succeeded that of the Levitical priesthood. When Paul claimed that they 'who preach the gospel should receive their living from the gospel' (1 Cor. 9:14—NIV), he was actually commenting upon the way in which the Levitical priesthood was sustained. 1 Corinthians 9:9 is a quotation from Deuteronomy 25:4: 'Thou shalt not muzzle the ox when he treadeth out the corn.' Paul also used Deuteronomy 25:4 in support of his claim that they who labour in the word and doctrine are worthy of 'double honour' (1 Tim. 5:17–18). 1 Corinthians 9:14 was also

followed by an appeal to Leviticus 6:16 when he asked: 'Do ye not know that they which minister about holy things live of the things of the temple? and they which wait at the altar are partakers with the altar? Even so hath the Lord ordained that they which preach the gospel should live of the gospel' (1 Cor. 9:13–14). As the sacrificial system of the Levitical priesthood had been abolished by the very sacrifice of Christ, obviously the only way the minister of the Gospel should live would be by 'storehouse' tithing.

By supporting an individual church, then, one not only supports the ministry of that church but provides funds for that particular church in turn to send the Gospel around the world. As Earl C. Wolf put it: 'Through my tithes and offerings I can preach the gospel in India, teach a Bible class in Taiwan, help the sick in a Swaziland hospital, translate the New Testament into the language of the Haitians or Indonesians, or love an orphaned child in Vietnam or Korea.' Carl Bates summed it up this way: 'God has always had a "place" for holy money to be put. In the Old Testament that place was the Tabernacle and the Temple. In the New Testament that place was and is the church. I have searched diligently to find a single instance in the Scriptures where the tithe was "designated". Offerings, yes, but not the tithe.' In other words, the tithe is to be *entrusted* to the Church that the Church may make the proper decisions as to its use.

4. *Cannot one's tithe be sent to any ministry that upholds God's word, like a missionary society, a Bible society, a Christian organisation or even a TV ministry?* In my view one cannot by-pass the Church in any way and be true to God's word. It is the Church which ought to support a missionary society or any other valid ministry. The Church is the fountainhead for all Christian enterprises. To give the tithe to the Church is to dignify the Church. To tithe directly to any other enterprise, however valid or 'sound', is robbing the 'storehouse' of its proper dignity.

If ever there was a time in which the dignity of the Church needs to be restored it is now. The Church has lost its credibility in the world. To give the actual tithe, God's tithe, to any organisation other than the Church is to perpetuate the loss of credibility which the Church has suffered. Were every Christian to tithe directly to the Church, it is my view that every Christian organisation which is owned of God would have more than ever.

I would agree with Carl Bates that 'offerings' beyond the tithe are an exception. For this way the *tithe* goes directly to the place where the Bible says it belongs. If somebody has an offering above the tithe he is inclined to place elsewhere than the Church, I could not find much objection. I would only hope that such a person takes seriously what needs there are in his own church first.

5. *What if one's tithe is so vast compared to that of other members in the church? Would not such a person's giving be a case of the 'tail wagging the dog'?* This kind of situation frequently emerges in the smaller churches. Sometimes a prosperous businessman's tithe is in excess of the rest of the membership combined. In a case like this it is a great test of that person's faith. It is the 'widow's mite' in reverse. As a person whose tithe is pennies needs to be assured that he or she should give nonetheless, so also does the wealthy man or woman. In a sense, it is a greater test. For as the poor man's tithe seems unimportant because it is so small, the wealthy man could give much less than his tithe and still make a church (if it is a small one) quite prosperous. The latter's temptation, then, is either 1. to withhold a portion of the tithe altogether or 2. spread it around. I believe that the tithe is the Lord's and that it should go directly to the church. It will not be a case of the tail wagging the dog. It is God's money and nobody else's.

A person whose tithe is a relatively large amount will no doubt be in a position to give vast amounts elsewhere. But he should be a 'churchman' first. He should set the example by dignifying the Church. God has placed him in a church, whatever its size, in His own secret will. The person whose tithe is larger than most should accept this. He must entrust his tithe to the Church he believes in. It is an act of great humility to entrust the Church with a vast amount of money. It is a test of faith, I say, that even exceeds that of the person whose income is small. But the fact remains that one is dealing not with one's own money but God's.

6. *What if one cannot afford to tithe?* The answer is, we cannot afford not to tithe. Who can afford to rob God? Those who rob God are impoverished and they perpetuate the melancholy state of the Church in the world today. J. Wilbur Chapman cited the only case he knew of in which a regular tither felt cheated in the end. A woman shared publicly with her church in a prayer meeting that God had failed her: 'Tomorrow I am to be discharged from the job I have held for many years. I do not have money saved up. I do not know what will become of me. For many years I have given to the Lord's cause; now, when I am old and not able to work, I face direst poverty and the shameful support of public charity. I feel that when I am laid off my job permanently tomorrow, I must tell God that He has not cared for me as He promised.'

Dr Chapman was invited to lunch the next day by a Christian businessman. This man told Dr Chapman how thrilled he was that his company was installing a pension plan for employees. 'Today we put this pension plan into effect, and the first person to go on retirement pay is a member of your church, Dr Chapman.' The church member was the woman who had complained the night before.

7. *What if I am the only tither in my church?* I have known of cases like this. It can be annoying to the person who alone is doing what God has commanded, and yet this should be seen as a wonderful example. First, what one does in this case is between that person and God. God sees what is happening. In the end that is all that really matters. You are the one who is enriched. Secondly, you should not be doing this for public recognition in any case. In my first pastorate I am quite sure that I was the only tither in the church. It was a church in the mountains of Tennessee and those mountaineers barely kept that little church going. If there was a need, they all pitched in and helped. But they weren't tithing. It was there that I

first heard the expression—for the church treasurer literally
said this to me: 'God will keep you humble, Brother Kendall,
and we will keep you poor.' I must say, they were true to their
word.

On a broader level there is nothing more trying than being
'the only one' who is apparently obedient. But we must avoid
the 'Elijah complex', as William Hendricks put it. 'I, even I
only, am left' (1 Kings 19:10) is an attitude that does not
endear us to God. 'How can ye believe, which receive honour
one of another, and seek not the honour that cometh from
God only?' (John 5:44). We must derive our joy from the
Lord Himself. What if no one else obeys? Am I better off if I
wait for others to do what *they* ought to do? What if nobody
else receives Christ as Saviour? Am I better off if I lose my
own soul? A day will come on which we shall *all* stand before
the judgment seat of Christ. Tithing will have nothing to do
with whether we are granted entrance into Heaven. But I
doubt very much that we will be sorry at God's judgment
that we were faithful to His word across the years. 'For we
must all appear before the judgment seat of Christ; that every
one may receive the things done in his body, according to
that he hath done, whether it be good or bad' (2 Cor. 5:10).

8. *Isn't tithing a hardship on the poor?* No, it is not. As someone
described it, 'The tithing plan is God's plan, and it is the
most fair and reasonable arrangement in the world.' The
poor man has to pay as much for food as the rich man. The
poor man has to pay the same for a gallon of petrol as the rich.
But if the poor man has a smaller income, he has a smaller
tithe. It does the poor man no favour to encourage him to
think that he is exempt from tithing. Why should he be
discriminated against? Tithing is a high privilege. God
dignifies us by saying that 10% of our income, whoever we
are, is His. That shows that I matter to God!

Tithing therefore gives dignity to every man. Tithing
breaks the socio-economic barrier. It cuts across any class
system. Tithing is for everyone, and the claim that 'the tithe
is the Lord's' puts every man—rich or poor, famous or

unknown—into a potentially intimate relationship with the Most High God. My 10% might be considerably less than someone else's, but that other person will not be more favoured than I in the sight of God. Tithing is a demonstration that God is no respecter of persons.

9. *Is it not a sin to tithe when you are in debt? Shouldn't we pay our honest debts first, then begin tithing?* No, to both questions. It is a sin, a high crime, not to pay your 'debt' to God—the tithe. It is His. On the second question, how much money do you really think that God would end up getting if every Christian waited until he or she was out of debt before they began tithing? Most Christians I know are in debt, and many are likely to be paying for a house or a car or a TV or whatever for a long time.

My own experience (as I related earlier) was that I was going deeper and deeper into debt until my wife and I started tithing. At that stage the 90% began to go so much further (don't ask me to explain it—I can't) toward paying my debts than I had been able to do with the entire 100% at the start.

By the way, notice that I said 'my wife and I'. Carl Bates once said: 'My wife and I are Storehouse Tithers.' It is a wonderful thing when both husband and wife feel the same way about this matter. It draws them closer to each other, they even work as a team.

10. *Should one keep personal records of one's own giving?* Yes. It is one way of certifying to yourself that, at the end of the year, your tithe actually equalled (or exceeded) 10% of your annual income. Besides it's good business. Many Christians are in debt simply because they have not learned how to handle money. Keeping records will help a lot. I also think that tithing can serve to motivate a person to be guarded in all *else* that he spends. For example, if you begin now to tithe and have not been doing so, you might find it a bit scary. 'How will we make it?' you might be asking. Giving God what is His may well serve to make you very careful in all other expenditures, and keeping records of *all* income and

expenditures is good business. Tithing might even be the means of teaching you how to handle all your money.

In America one has the opportunity to deduct one's gifts to the church from one's income tax, therefore keeping records is essential. This is not so in Britain. A British Christian therefore has an opportunity to prove his earnestness in a way that Americans might not. For in America the 'tax deduction' has been a supplementary motivation for some to tithe. This is somewhat a pity. I sometimes wonder what would happen to giving in America if Uncle Sam suddenly said, 'No more tax deductions based on giving to the Church.' It seems in fact that in the United States there has been a trend toward this anyway. The government is making it more and more difficult for ordinary citizens. The time may come when Americans will prove their love for the Lord Jesus Christ by giving without the privilege of tax deductions. But this has always been true in Britain. I think that Christians in Britain have a glorious opportunity to set a high standard of giving to Americans and the world when it is realised they have no such luxury as a tax deduction insofar as gifts to the Church are concerned. What the British can do, however, is to sign a 'deed of covenant' which allows the *church* (not the individual giver) to reclaim a proportion of revenue from the government. Every Christian in Britain should take full advantage of this for the Church's sake. The British method works out to the advantage of the church or charity, whereas the American method works out to the advantage of the individual. In either case I would certainly recommend taking full advantage of the regulations of the law and in both cases the keeping of records.

11. *What is the best procedure for the tither who has difficulty in handling money and 'making ends meet'? What if he finds that he has no money left after he has bought his groceries and paid his bills?* The best procedure for *anyone* is to *begin* with tithe. *Take it off the top*. Put the tithe at the top of the list. If your monthly income is £400, then lay £40 aside and begin to budget your expenditure on the basis of £360. It is as simple as that. If your weekly

income is £50, then lay £5 aside and operate from then on on £45. If your income is £1200, then lay £120 aside and go from there on £1080. Remember: what was laid aside is 'holy unto the Lord' and must not be touched. It is the Lord's and must be set completely aside until the first day of the week (1 Cor. 16:2).

12. *Should the tithe be paid weekly or monthly?* If you are paid weekly, then pay your tithe every Sunday. If you are paid monthly, pay your tithe the first Sunday after you have been paid. If you are a farmer or are in business for yourself, you no doubt have learned the discipline of handling money. In some cases it might be good to 'estimate' the tithe (if you have funds in the meantime) until you can clarify matters once you know how much money you have taken in. This way you can give fairly regularly for the good of the Church.

13. *Should teenagers or even children tithe?* Yes, if they have income. The best time to learn is when you are young. I treasure my own experience (as I have said earlier). Joan Barnett once addressed some young people: 'Teenagers, I started tithing when I received that all-important pay cheque from that exciting first job. I was so appreciative of that job, I was determined God would get the first of that money. You surely realise God expects you to tithe.' God honours young people too!

14. *Should students who have a grant tithe?* This sort of thing will vary, but I would not regard a grant that has been designated for tuition as income. This is quite different. A grant has been given for a specific purpose. But in the case in which the total grant exceeds the amount required for tuition and lodging I would challenge the student to tithe the 'net' as a business man would do.

15. *Should one tithe what one has been reimbursed for as expenses?* No, for that is not income.

16. *Should one tithe one's retirement pension?* Certainly. And yet some point out that if you have tithed the gross of your pay across the years, your retirement income has already been tithed! This is true up to a point. But usually the employer or the government adds to the fund, moreover the plan does not stop until you die; therefore, there is no way to calculate how much of your own money will come back to you.

Some may think this is a trifling question, if not foolish. But it worries a lot of people. I would leave you with God. 'Work out your own salvation with fear and trembling' (Philip. 2:12). I would certainly think that the Christian would want to tithe to his last breath, and it would seem to me that any pension is income.

'E'en down to old age all my people shall prove
    My sovereign, eternal, unchangeable love;
And when hoary hairs shall their temples adorn,
    Like lambs they shall still in my bosom be borne.'

17. *Surely questions like these smack of legalism. What does it matter whether one literally keeps records to be sure one has paid an actual 10%? Isn't this really being legalistic?* Perhaps. It most certainly could prove detrimental to one's spirit, especially if one got into a legalistic rut. This is why I stressed the matter of assurance before God apart from the Law. We are saved utterly and wholly and absolutely by the grace of God. Tithing will not help a person get to Heaven. It will not save you. It will not help you to become a Christian. If I believe anything at all, I believe that we are saved by grace alone through faith alone in Christ alone. Tithing adds nothing to that.

I equally believe however that every Christian has an opportunity to show gratitude to God. Sanctification is voluntary obedience. The more we shun sin and temptation, the more grateful we appear. Billy Sunday once said that the reason Christians fall into sin is that they treat temptation like strawberry shortcake rather than a rattlesnake. If you are married, you do not want your husband or your wife

treating the marriage vow loosely. If your wife wants to act
flippantly with another man, I don't think you would like
that very much. Is she being 'legalistic' to be *care-ful* as well as
faithful?

We are married to Christ (Rom. 7:4). If He does not care
whether we are careful or faithful to Him, we would well
wonder if He cares about us at all! But He does care. He loved
us so much that He gave His life for us. He loves us so much
that He watches our every move right now. He dignifies us by
taking notice of our every move. We are motivated to live
godly lives when we realise this. The more careful we are, the
more pleasing we are to Him. We are careful to please Him
because He died for us. The matter of tithing is a way of
showing we care. The matter of keeping records is a way of
showing how particular we are. Samuel Young said: 'The
primary motivation for giving is the cross of Jesus Christ. If
that does not move us, nothing else will for very long.' Dr
Young also said: 'When the giving is wrong, the living is not
quite right.' I do not believe we displease God by being
careful that we turn *all* of the tithe over to Him.

18. *But isn't there still a danger of being legalistic?* Yes. But not a
very serious danger. When you realise you are saved and
accepted by God regardless of whether or not you tithe, it is
not likely that legalism will take a 'front seat'. The danger is
this. You must never think that tithing counts for righteousness. It does not. For if you think that it does, you give God
further grounds to chasten you. This is precisely why I stated
earlier that God blesses us on the 'apparent condition' of
obedience. He stoops to where we are to motivate us. But it
does not follow that we can bargain with God on the basis of
tithing. We can never do this, and should we *think* it, we must
put it out of our minds at once! God did not absolutely and
categorically promise a particular kind of blessing. Paul
merely said, 'God is able' (2 Cor. 9:8). Malachi said, 'See if I
will not' bless you (Mal. 3:10—NIV). These verses are
carefully worded in order to protect the sovereignty and
freedom of God.

A legalistic rut may emerge in two ways: 1. If we should secretly hope or believe that tithing counts for righteousness. We must see our own tithing as 'filthy rags' (Is. 64:6). Should God's blessing happen to coincide with our obedience, we should not ascribe this phenomenon directly to our obedience but to the kindness of God who enabled us to obey! 2. If we divide our gross income by 10% to the nearest percentage point so that we become afraid to give too much or too little. Whereas we should be careful, we don't have to be ridiculous.

19. *But is it not possible to slip into an 'afraid not to give' syndrome? If we do, should we not stop giving until we are over that?* It is certainly true that one can slip into the 'afraid not to give' syndrome. But what on earth is there that we *ever* do that is not beset with that problem? We may be afraid to miss a church service lest they have an unusually good one; I am afraid not to prepare a sermon adequately for I don't trust my ability to preach many times spontaneously; I am afraid not to keep my car rather full of petrol for I may need the car when stations are closed; I am afraid not to be friendly at all times for I don't want someone to get needlessly hurt; I am afraid not to eat properly or sleep enough lest I become needlessly vulnerable to germs. Do I abandon these fears just to prove to myself I refuse to be in a rut? I am not better off if I do. But it seems that when it comes to our finances we can get very vulnerable indeed to the temptation to stop giving. This is probably why John Wesley said that the last part of a man to be converted is his wallet. Martin Luther said, 'Every man needs two conversions: the first his heart, the second of his wallet!'

The 'afraid not to give' syndrome on the whole is a healthy fear. It is a fear based on faith. Certainly it is possible for a selfish motive to slip in alongside a valid concern, but on the whole we do what we know in our hearts is right—whether we feel like it or not. Just because a selfish fear competes with a valid concern is not good enough reason to abandon the enterprise altogether! Perhaps when I am tempted not to

prepare a sermon as carefully as usual, a parallel fear that my
congregation will notice this will emerge; am I better off (or
are they?) simply because I refused to be bothered about
this? Sometimes the devil wins a victory simply because we
think we have to prove ourselves, when it is only because a
temptation we are ashamed of vies for our attention. That
temptation must be ignored, resisted, lest I get distracted
from what is right and responsible.

When I give because I am 'afraid not to', I am never sorry
later. It simply means that my being 'afraid not to' was a
responsible concern after all, not a petty, selfish motivation.

20. *If I have not been tithing, it means I am 'behind' in my tithes. This
means I am deeply in debt—to God. Should I pay 'back tithes'?* No.
Begin now. When God forgives, He forgets. Confess your sin
of not tithing. Accept your forgiveness (1 John 1:9). Don't
look back. Go on. But don't repeat the same sin. Go and sin
no more. God forgives and keeps forgiving, true, but He is not
to be mocked. 'Be not deceived; God is not mocked: for
whatsoever a man soweth, that shall he also reap' (Gal. 6:7).
If you are truly sorry, however, accept your forgiveness and
go forward.

On the other hand, if you have accumulated funds, you
might, like Zacchaeus, want to do something. He was so
overcome with gratitude that he wanted to give away half of
his goods (Luke 19:8). Perhaps you have been blessed by
God financially despite not being a tither. You should feel
very humble and grateful. My advice is as that given above,
go on—don't look back. But if you wanted to give a 'token'
offering of gratitude to God to His church, I would understand. You have nothing to lose by that.

I close this final chapter with this. Begin tithing *now*. I
cannot be more serious when I say begin at once. Place your
tithe of the current month or week in your church next
Sunday. Cultivate a habit that you will not break the rest of
your life.

Conclusion

W. A. Criswell tells us the story about the pastor who was asked, 'How many church members do you have?' The answer was, 'One hundred fifty.' The pastor was further asked, 'How many of them are tithers?' The pastor replied, 'One hundred fifty.' In astonishment the enquirer exclaimed, 'What! All one hundred fifty, the entire church, are tithers?' 'Yes indeed,' said the pastor. 'About fifty of them bring the tithe to the storehouse, and God collects it from the rest.'

In the end 'we do not cheat God,' concludes Dr Criswell. 'I can either give it to him in a deeply spiritual act of worship, or He can collect it. In either case, God gets His own.' The melancholy fact remains however that the storehouse is robbed when we do not bring the tithe to it. God gets it but it does not follow that the storehouse gets it. When God is robbed He has His own way of collecting it from us. How does God collect the tithe? 'Ye are cursed with a curse: for ye have robbed me, even this whole nation' (Mal. 3:9). That is not the way God wants to collect it. He takes no delight in showing His displeasure with us.

It is of great comfort to know that God is serious about the matter of tithing. It is of no small consolation that He actually cares what I do with my money. When I think that God owns 'the cattle on a thousand hills' (Ps. 50:10) but still cares for me so much that He takes notice of my own money, this gives me a very secure feeling. Because it also means He notices when I am in financial need. He really cares!

God cares so much that He meets us where we are. The proof of this is His way of motivating us. Just as we motivate our children to do what they in fact must do because it is best for them, so God stoops to our weakness to lead us. After we have done what He sought to get us to do we are thankful to Him as eventually we are to our concerned parents.

There are various levels of motivation. In other words, the reason *why* we actually give will reveal whether we are giving begrudgingly or cheerfully. Our hearts can play tricks on us. 'The heart is deceitful above all things, and desperately wicked; who can know it?' (Jer. 17:9). Checking out our own motives can be a rather painful thing. Who can know what our motives really are?

I should like to list five levels of motivation insofar as our giving is concerned. It would seem that the first two levels come under the category of giving with a grudge, the last two with cheerfulness, the one in the middle being borderline.

1. *Giving in the light of tax advantages.* This applies in some countries, particularly in America. The Bible alone should provide our motive for giving to the Church. When we let governmental regulations serve as the basis of motivation, surely this means that we are being impelled from the lowest level. One most certainly ought to take advantage of such regulations while they are in existence (as the British Christian ought to give through the deed of covenant), but if such serves as the reason for giving it is quite sad indeed. How would one know if he is being motivated at this level? Answer: if you knew that the government would not recognise your gift, would you give the exact amount, as often, anyway? Perhaps the only way finally to know whether one's motive is at this level is to live in another country, with different tax laws, and see whether one's individual giving decreases.

2. *Giving in the light of the Church's survival.* Some give to a church in order to keep it barely going—that is, to pay the bills (including the pastor's salary). It may be argued that those who do this can do so cheerfully because they feel very good that their money is so desperately needed. Some of us can get a very righteous feeling when we know we are saving

a sinking ship. But this is surely disgraceful when we are talking about the Church for which Christ died! It is treating God's own Church patronisingly as if the Church is lucky to have our support. This then is hardly cheerful giving.

3. *Giving in the light of God's possible chastening.* This is borderline. It most certainly is not giving cheerfully. If anything, it is giving begrudgingly. And yet it is a higher level than what we have seen above because it is at least given in faith. For one does this realising that God is involved. The two levels above virtually leave God out. To the extent one gives in the light of God taking notice, this is done in a measure of faith. Moreover, the fear of God's chastening is not to be dismissed as an entirely bad motive. Most of us have experienced this, and it is the only motivation some of us can get in touch with when we are not living as devotedly to Christ as we ought. The fear of chastening has kept many a child of God from falling into sin. Who among us has not known this? If our Lord Himself uses this as a motivation we must not take it lightly. 'Sin no more, lest a worse thing come unto thee' (John 5:14).

4. *Giving in the light of God's possible blessing.* When the Apostle Paul said for us to give not grudgingly but cheerfully it was in the context of the promise of blessing. 'Every man according as he purposeth in his heart, so let him give; not grudgingly, or of necessity: for God loveth a cheerful giver. And God is able to make all grace abound toward you; that ye, always having all sufficiency in all things, may abound to every good work' (2 Cor. 9:7–8). The promise of the blessing was to cheer us up when we are tempted not to give! Paul did not mean that we should only give when we are in a cheerful mood—much less give such a small amount that it will not interfere with our good mood—but give because God takes notice! How does He take notice of our giving? By showing it with blessing. 'Prove me now herewith, saith the Lord of hosts, if I will not open you the windows of heaven, and pour

you out a blessing, that there shall not be room enough to receive it' (Mal. 3:10).

5. *Giving in the light of God's glory.* This is the highest level of all. To glorify God. It is the 'but if not' faith (Dan. 3:18). It is to give God what is His because it is His! It is to tithe because it is right. It is, as it were, even to forget the promise of blessing. One gives to God out of sheer gratitude. One gives because he or she has *already* been blessed. To be blessed further by doing what one delights to do already is almost too much! In other words, when one gives to glorify God it is truly not letting your right hand know what your left hand is doing (Matt. 6:23). It is adopting in advance the attitude that 'we are unprofitable servants: we have done that which was our duty to do' (Luke 17:10).

Tithing in any case does more for us spiritually than it does at any material level. There is no doubt about this. It releases the Spirit. It taps other resources in our inheritance in Christ that otherwise had been shut tight. This is why Adrian Rogers has said, 'The purpose of tithing is to prove God.' For tithing is 'His way for us to *develop faith* in Him.' Dr Rogers tells the story of a man who made his sons work in the cornfields while other boys were out in the swimming hole, playing in the fields and doing other things. Someone remonstrated with the man and said, 'Why do you make those boys work so hard in your cornfields? You don't need all that corn.' The man answered: 'Sir, I'm not raising corn, I'm raising boys.'

When William C. Burns was leaving Scotland for China someone rather cynically said to him: 'I suppose you are going to China to convert the Chinese?' 'No,' replied Burns. 'I'm going to China to glorify God.' If someone says to us, 'I suppose you are tithing in order to be blessed,' we must reply: 'No. I am tithing to glorify God.' William C. Burns however did under God convert many Chinese. Do not be surprised when you are blessed. It is God's way.

In the meantime everybody is blessed. You are blessed. The Church is blessed. The nation is blessed. It was a nation that robbed God in Malachi's day. It is likewise a nation that shall be blessed when the people of God do not break trust with Him. 'Blessed is that nation whose God is the Lord' (Ps. 33:12). 'Righteousness exalteth a nation: but sin is a reproach to any people' (Prov. 14:34). When the people of God are not a tithing people, everybody loses. But when the people of God are dedicated to His glory, everybody wins.